Fodor's POCKET

P9-CDB-068

shanghai

second edition

Excerpted from *Fodor's China*

fodor's travel publications
new york • toronto • london • sydney • auckland
www.fodors.com

contents

maps

on the road with fodor's

THE MORE YOU KNOW BEFORE YOU GO, the better your trip will be. Shanghai's most fascinating small museum or its best restaurant could be just around the corner from your hotel, but if you don't know it's there, it might as well be across the globe. That's where this guidebook and our Web site, Fodors.com, come in. Our editors work hard to give you useful, on-target information. Their efforts begin with finding the best contributors—people with good judgment and broad travel experience—the people you'd poll for tips yourself if you knew them.

Laurel Back has traveled and lived in more than 30 countries around the world. While working on her Masters, Laurel decided to tackle a Cultural Study of China. Laurel has now traveled twice to China and has participated in many cultural orientations with Chinese exchange students. She updated Practical Information.

Paul Davidson, who updated Shanghai, also covered eastern and southwest China for *Fodor's China*. He currently lives in Yokohama, Japan.

Don't Forget to Write

Keeping a travel guide fresh and up-to-date is a big job. So we love your feedback—positive and negative—and follow up on all suggestions. Contact the *Pocket Shanghai* editor at editors@fodors.com or c/o Fodor's, 280 Park Avenue, New York, New York 10017. And have a wonderful trip!

Karen Cure
Editorial Director

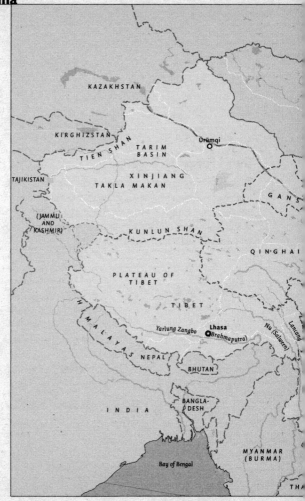

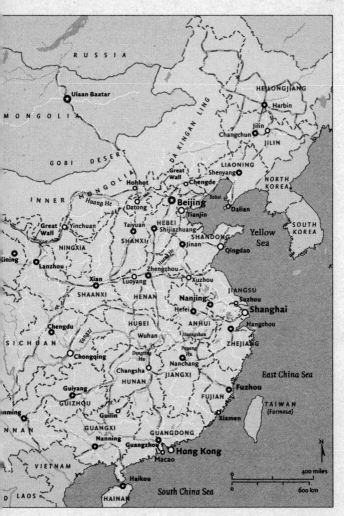

shanghai

In This Chapter

Updated by Paul Davidson

introducing shanghai

SHANGHAI, LITERALLY, THE "CITY ON THE SEA," in the 1990s became —and still is—the center of China's economic resurgence. Shanghai's allure begins with its glamorous past of sepia-lighted halls, opium dens, and French villas. A gathering of cultures, it once was a place where rich taipans walked the same streets as gamblers, prostitutes, and beggars, and Europeans fleeing the Holocaust lived alongside Chinese intellectuals and revolutionaries.

The Communist Party was born here, but its strict tenets could not stifle the city's unflagging internationalism, which was determined at its creation. Although the nation has a history thousands of years old, Shanghai itself could be called a new Chinese invention. Lying on the Yangzi River delta, it marks the point where Asia's longest and most important river completes its 5,500-km (3,400-mi) journey to the Pacific. Until 1842 Shanghai's location made it merely a small fishing village. After the first Opium War, the British named Shanghai a treaty port, forcing the city's opening to foreign involvement.

The village was soon turned into a city carved up into autonomous concessions administered by the British, French, and Americans, all independent of Chinese law. Each colonial presence brought with it its particular culture, architecture, and society. Although Shanghai had its own walled Chinese city, many native residents still chose to live in the foreign settlements. Thus began a mixing of cultures that shaped Shanghai's openness to Western influence. Shanghai became an important industrial center and trading port that attracted not only foreign businesspeople (60,000 by the 1930s) but also Chinese migrants from other parts of the country.

In its heyday, Shanghai was the place to be—it had the best art, the greatest architecture, and the strongest business in Asia. With dance halls, brothels, glitzy restaurants, international clubs, and even a foreign-run racetrack, Shanghai was a city that catered to every whim of the rich. But poverty ran alongside opulence, and many of the lower-class Chinese provided the cheap labor that kept the city running.

The Paris of the East became known as a place of vice and indulgence. Amid this glamour and degradation the Communist Party held its first meeting in 1921. The thirties and forties saw invasion and war. The city weathered Japanese raids and then the victory of the Communists in 1949 over the Nationalists, after which foreigners left the country. Closed off from the outside world with which it had become so comfortable, Shanghai fell into a deep sleep. Fashion, music, and romance gave way to uniformity and the stark reality of Communism.

Today Shanghai has once again become one of China's most open cities ideologically, socially, culturally, and economically, striving to return to the internationalism that defined it before the Revolution. Shanghai's path to this renewed prominence began in 1990 when China's leader, Deng Xiaoping, chose it as the engine of the country's commercial renaissance, aiming to rival Hong Kong by 2010. If China is a dragon, he said, Shanghai is its head. Today the city is all about business. Having embraced competition and a market-driven economy in just a few years, it now hosts the nation's stock market, accounts for one-sixth of the country's gross national product, and houses the most important industrial base in the nation.

Today Shanghai draws more parallels to New York City than Paris—a true city, it is laid out on a grid (unlike sprawling Beijing), and with a population of 16 million, it is one of the world's most crowded urban areas. Nowhere else in China can you feel the same pulse, dynamism, and enthusiasm.

The Shanghainese have a reputation for being sharp, open-minded, glamorous, sophisticated, and business-oriented, and they're convinced they have the motivation and attitude to achieve their place as China's powerhouse. Far away from Beijing's watchful political eyes, yet supported by state officials who call Shanghai their hometown, the people have a freedom to grow that their counterparts in the capital don't enjoy. That ambition can be witnessed firsthand across Shanghai's Huangpu River, which joins the Yangzi at the northern outskirts of the city. Here, Shanghai's most important project is being built—Pudong New Area, China's 21st-century financial, economic, and commercial center. "The east side of the river," is home to Shanghai's new stock market building, the tallest hotel in the world, the city's new international airport, and, soon, the world's tallest building. And rising from land that just a few years ago was dominated by rice paddies is the city's pride and joy, the Oriental Pearl Tower—a gaudy, flashing, spaceshiplike pillar, the tallest in Asia.

During the last decade, Puxi, (the west side of the river), has also gone through staggering change. Charming old houses are making way for shiny high-rises. The population is moving from alley housing in the city center to spanking-new apartments in the suburbs. Architecturally spectacular new museums and theaters are catching the world's attention. Foreign shopping centers and malls are popping up on every corner. Residents walk down to their favorite store only to find it's been torn down to make room for a new architectural wonder. In 1987 there were about 150 high-rise buildings in the city. Today there are more than 1,500, and the number continues to grow. Shanghai is reputed to be home to one-fifth of all the world's construction cranes.

Shanghai's open policy has also made the city the hot new attraction for foreign investors. As millions of dollars pour in, especially to Pudong, Shanghai has again become home to tens of thousands of expatriates. Foreign influence has made today's Shanghai a consumer heaven. Domestic stores rub shoulders with the boutiques of Louis Vuitton, Christian Dior, and Ralph Lauren. Newly made businessmen battle rush-hour traffic in their Mercedes and Lexus cars. Young people keep the city up till the wee hours as they dance the night away in clubs blasting the latest techno grooves. And everyone walks around with a de rigueur mobile phone or pager attached to his or her belt.

In Shanghai it's all about image; it's not surprising, then, that the Shanghainese enjoy one of the highest living standards in China. Higher salaries and higher buildings, more business and more entertainment—they all define the fast-paced lives of China's most cosmopolitan and open people.

PLEASURES AND PASTIMES

ANTIQUES MARKETS

Chairman Mao alarm clocks, calligraphy scrolls, porcelain, jade pieces, valuable coins, old Chinese locks, and a great number of fake antiques are spread carefully on tables that line the streets on a weekly, sometimes daily basis. Beware of rip-offs: if you're seriously searching for antiques, it's best to get a local who speaks English to bargain for you while you wait unseen for the right price.

ARCHITECTURE

Shanghai's history is eclectic, and so is its architecture. Although significant portions of the city are making way for skyscrapers, some of what has defined its original charm still exists. From the neoclassicism of the Bund to the art deco of the French Concession to the quaint Chinese alleys of the old city, a walk through town can evoke memories of romantic old Shanghai. But hurry: as you read this, old buildings are being torn down.

The high points, literally, of new architecture are the skyscraping Jinmao Tower and Oriental Pearl Tower in Pudong, both of which have opened sky-high observatories.

EARLY MORNING

At six in the morning, no matter where you are in China, everyone is up and outside buying their daily vegetables, fruits, meats, eggs, and noodles at the local market. Vendors are out steaming, frying, boiling, and selling breakfast snacks to people on their way to work. Men and women practice tai chi in parks, along rivers, and in some unlikely places—the steps of a movie theater, an empty alley, the side entrance of a hotel.

TEA HOUSES

On the fourth floor of a department store, on cobblestone streets, and in subway stations—tea houses are to China as cafes are to France. Relax, chat, and meditate over a pot of Oolong while sampling dried fruit snacks.

PORTRAITS

DOING BUSINESS IN CHINA

If you're a business traveler in China, you probably still feel like a pioneer, even though it's been almost 20 years since Deng Xiaoping launched the "open door" policy and started inviting foreign investment into the previously isolated country. "We are learning how to compete in the market economy, and we need foreign expertise," a Chinese official or enterprise manager might tell you. But don't be misled into believing that you can come in with a plan this week and sign a contract next week, or that Western-style efficiency will be welcome in a joint venture with a Chinese company.

The Chinese, as every foreign business traveler quickly learns, have an elaborate unwritten code of rules that apply to every aspect of business, from negotiating the contract to selling the product.

A good way to prepare yourself is to read Sun Tze's *The Art of War*. The true author of this Chinese classic is unknown, but the best guess is that it was written by a brilliant military strategist who lived sometime around the 4th century BC. Sun Tze's basic principle held that moral strength and intellectual faculty were the decisive factors in battle, and today, these are the guiding factors in negotiating business deals. Not that you're dealing with adversaries. But from the days when the first foreign firms began to eye China's vast potential market of 1.2 billion consumers, the Chinese quickly realized that they had something the world wanted, so why not assure themselves a share in the capital that foreign ventures were sure to generate?

In recent years, a number of major Western companies have played hardball with Chinese officials and held their own. In 1996 for example, Disney was in discussions with the central government about distributing movies, selling merchandise, and building theme parks in China when Liu Jianzhong, director of the Film Bureau in the Ministry of Radio, Film and Television, warned that there might be no final approval for these projects if a Disney subsidiary went ahead with production of a film about the Dalai Lama, the Tibetan spiritual leader who is considered an enemy by the Chinese government. Disney refused to stop the film from being made and was blacklisted all over China. By 1999, Shanghai was in deep competition against Hong Kong wooing Disney to set up a Disneyland.

According to *The Art of War*, you sometimes have to yield a city or give up ground in order to gain a more valuable objective. Although it might seem a good idea in the short run to bow to ideological pressure from China, it is probably best for a company's long-term goals and international image to hold out. There is dissension today within the ranks of China's government, and attempts to appease the authorities who make demands today may backfire if these people fall out of favor domestically, or if America's political relations with China deteriorate.

Furthermore, though the Chinese authorities may insist that their politics are none of our business, the lack of a clear rule of law in China can work against conducting business here. On a number of occasions business people have found themselves arrested and detained on trumped-up or nonexistent charges following a disagreement with a local partner or government authority over terms. Often the disagreement has to do with a city or provincial ministry's wanting an unreasonable share in the company. It is to the advantage of all foreigners living or spending time in China to push for political reforms that would incorporate due process of law.

This is all part of pioneering. In a country that had almost no modern roads 20 years ago, there are now huge swathes of concrete everywhere—and vehicles to run on them. According to World Bank figures, China's economy, before the Asian contagion, was the third fastest-growing in the world, with an annual average rate of 9.2% between 1978 and 1996. (Only Thailand and South Korea are ahead.) From being a country with virtually no capital, it has moved to among the top six nations in the world in terms of foreign exchange reserves. The people in the cities wear designer fashions, and construction cranes loom above almost every city or village street. Some observers think that as the market economy grows, a measure of democratic reform will come. The Chinese people themselves are likely to demand a freer flow of information, if only to help them make financial decisions. In early 1997, for example, there was talk in China of a desperate need for the domestic news media to report responsibly and independently on the wild gyrations of the Shenzhen and Shanghai stock markets, so that the 21 million Chinese who own corporate equities can monitor their investments.

In spite of the economic reforms, this is still a centrally planned system called "socialism with Chinese characteristics." It is still a society with a thousand years of practice at handling foreign traders. Here are some fundamentals you should know before you go:

YOUR TEAM: If you're new to the place, retain the services of a China consultant who knows the language and has a strong track record. The nonprofit U.S. China Business Council (1818 N St. NW, Suite 200, Washington, DC 20036, tel. 202/429–0340, fax 202/775–2476, with additional offices in Hong Kong, Beijing, and Shanghai) is a good source for consulting services, referrals, and other information. Choose your own translator who will look out for your interests.

Know who you'll be meeting with in China, and send people with corresponding titles. The Chinese are very hierarchical and will be offended if you send a low-level manager to meet a minister. All of this ties into the all-important and intricate concept of "face," which can best be explained as the need to preserve dignity and standing.

Don't bring your spouse on the trip, unless he or she is involved in the business. Otherwise the Chinese will think your trip is really a vacation.

ATTITUDES TOWARD WOMEN: The Chinese will take a woman seriously if she has an elevated title and acts serious. Women will find themselves under less pressure than men to hang out at the karaoke until the wee hours. This is partly because the party list might include prostitutes. (A woman will also avoid the trap that Chinese local partners sometimes lay to get rid of an out-of-favor foreign manager. They'll have a prostitute pick him up, then get the police to catch him so that he can be banished from the country for a sexual offense.)

BUSINESS CARDS: Bring more than you ever thought you'd need. Consult a translator before you go and have cards made with your name and the name of your company in Chinese characters on the reverse side.

THE GREETING: When you are introduced to someone in China, immediately bow your head slightly and offer your business card, with two hands. In the same ceremonious fashion accept your colleague's business card, which will likely be turned up to show an Anglicized name.

Be there on time. The Chinese are very punctual. When you are hosting a banquet, arrive at the restaurant at least 30 minutes before your guests.

THE MEETING: Don't make plans for the rest of the day, or evening, or tomorrow or the next day. And don't be in a rush to get home. Meetings can go on for days, weeks, whatever it takes to win concessions. Meetings will continue over a lavish lunch, a lavish dinner that includes many toasts with mao tai, and a long night at a karaoke, consuming XO cognac from a showy bottle. To keep in shape for the lengthy meetings, learn the art of throwing a shot of mao tai onto the floor behind you instead of drinking it down when your host says "ganbei." (Chances are he is not really drinking either.)

GIFTS AND BRIBES: Yes, a local official might ask you to get his child into a foreign university or buy your venture partner a fleet of BMWs. A few years ago a survey by the Independent Commission Against Corruption in Hong Kong found that corrupt business practices may represent 3%–5% of the cost of doing business in China, a factor that respondents (Hong Kong firms) claimed was bearable and not a disincentive. However, the Chinese government has been campaigning against corruption and business fraud.

American companies have the added constraint of the Foreign Corrupt Practices Act, which prohibits offering or making payments to officials of foreign countries. The law can be a good excuse for not paying bribes. However, you may find yourself faced with a great many arbitrary fees to be paid to the city and county for everything from your business license to garbage collection. It is hard to avoid paying these.

To win friends in a small but legal way, give small gifts to the people you meet. Bring a shipment of such items as pens, paperweights, and T-shirts emblazoned with your company logo. And, before you leave town, host a banquet for all of the people who have entertained you.

COMMUNICATION: Gestures that seem insignificant on the surface will help make or break your efforts to gain entry into China. Escort a departing visitor to the elevator as a way of giving him face, for example. To make a visitor feel particularly esteemed, walk him all the way to the front door of the building. And don't "have other plans" when your Chinese associates invite you out. As in many Asian countries, personal relationships are more important than the contract. The people you are dealing with may not tell you what they really want from a partnership with you until you're out eating and drinking.

There are many ways of saying "no" that may sound like "yes" to foreigners. If you hear that your proposal "is under study" or has arrived at "an inconvenient time," start preparing a new one.

A manager of a local factory in search of a foreign venture partner might tell you that the deal can be done, but that doesn't mean it will be. Make sure you meet with the officials in charge of your sector in the city, those who have the authority to approve the deal. If someone says he has to get the boss's approval, you should have a hearing with the boss—even if it means getting your boss there on the next flight to meet with his counterpart.

Early on, you may be asked to sign a "letter of intent." This document is not legally binding; it serves more as an expression of seriousness. But the principles in the letter, which look like ritual statements to the Westerner because they lack specific detail, may be invoked later if your Chinese partner has a grudge against you. He'll say you have not lived up to the spirit of mutual cooperation and benefit initially agreed upon.

HOW TO COMPROMISE: You will have to give your Chinese partner something he wants. He might, for instance, want your capital to go into lines of business other than what you had in mind. You might have to agree to this if establishing a presence in China is important to your business. Take the example of John C. Portman III, vice chairman of the Atlanta-based architecture firm John Portman & Associates. Portman spent the early 1980s courting the Shanghai government. Besides volunteering suggestions for redeveloping the city, he set up a trading company that brought an exhibition of goods from Shanghai to Atlanta. Not his usual line of business, but in the end the friendships he'd cultivated netted his company the coveted contract to design and develop the $200-million Shanghai Centre, which houses the Portman Ritz-Carlton Hotel, and China now accounts for about half of the company's total business.

Know when to be flexible, but for important details such as who actually has control of the venture and its operations, hold out, even if it takes a year or more. There are ways to make sure of who is really in charge of a joint venture, even though for matters of face and power the Chinese partner will probably want to provide the person with the loftiest title. You will also want to own the controlling share, because it means quality control, profitability, and decision-making power over matters for which your company is legally liable. Often an inside deal is worked out, whereby the foreign party provides the general manager, who actually is in charge of day-to-day operations, while the Chinese partner brings in the chairman, who works with a board of directors and has authority only over broad policy issues.

Don't go to China and tell your prospective partner you want to start production by a certain date. Expect your Chinese associates to drive their hardest bargain just when you thought it was safe to go home. They know that once rumors of a concluded negotiation become public, you will not be able to back down from the deal without having to make difficult explanations to your investors and headquarters.

Demand that your contract include an arbitration clause, which stipulates that if a dispute arises the matter will be tried by an arbitrator, preferably in the United States or a third country. However, even in China, there are arbitration centers that comply with international standards and are well ahead of the court system.

BEING THERE: Saddled with 50 employees from the state-owned enterprise and you don't even have a customer in China? That's the way things have been done. You will have to make changes slowly and be prepared to train people for new skills. Profits may be equally slow to roll in, but remember the corporate axiom that has become the main China strategy: We're in it for the long haul.

If you're trying to break into the China market with a product or service, learn more about the consumers you're targeting through a focus study. These have become popular among prospective consumers, who have proved willing to sit through sessions lasting as long as three hours. (Focus panels generally last only 40 minutes in the United States.) Test the name in different cities, because meaning can vary according to the local language. As the *Economist Intelligence Unit* reported recently, one company had a name for a butter product that meant "yellow oil" in one city, "engine oil" in another, and "cow fat" in a third.

THE LAW IN CHINA: China works on civil law—that is, laws are passed by the National People's Congress and implemented. Quickly. Hong Kong's legal structure is based on common law (the same as Britain's and the United States'), which develops through judicial decisions (case law). The heart of Hong Kong's existence, "One Country, Two Systems," is that both judicial systems exist side by side. But sometimes they clash in China, particularly when it comes to business. In 1999, 29 Hong Kong businessmen were being detained in China. About half languished under house arrest in hotels or actually behind bars because a business deal had gone sour. Many actually are citizens of other countries. The aggrieved party, which sometimes turns out to be officialdom, just grabs the person as a hostage until the money, which they see as theirs, is handed over. In at least two cases, the hostages were not released even after court rulings in China so ordered.

WILL FENG SHUI HELP YOUR PROSPECTS? The 7,000-year-old art of placing objects in harmony with the environment and the elements is virtually mandatory in Hong Kong and Taiwan—it always had a stronger influence in southern China. In other areas, it's officially considered feudalist superstitious nonsense, but of course, if it facilitates business. . . . If there's any doubt in your mind, by all means call a geomancer.

While China speeds along toward overtaking the United States as the world's largest economy—the World Bank forecasts that will happen in the year 2020—any number of factors may make or break your efforts to reap some of the benefits of this dizzying growth. Barring serious political upheaval, you'll probably want to stay here and make constant—i.e., day-to-day—adaptations to the changing demands of the market. Like armies, companies in China have to figure out when to advance their presence, when to scale back, when to retreat to another location. And with each new strategy, be prepared to negotiate, feast, and sing karaoke songs.

BOOKS AND VIDEOS

BOOKS

For general overviews of Chinese history from the 1600s to the present, start with *The Search for Modern China* (Jonathan Spence, Norton, New York, 1990) or *The Rise of Modern China* (Immanuel Hsu, Oxford University Press, New York, 4th edition, 1990). To explore deeper roots, with essays on specific cultural topics, read *An Introduction to Chinese Civilization* (John Meskill, ed., D.C. Heath, Boston, 1973).

A number of memoirs have been published in recent years that provide not only personal stories, but also intimate windows on China's vast socioeconomic changes. *Wild Swans: Three Daughters of China* (Chang Jung, Simon & Schuster, New York, 1991) covers much of the 20th century in its look at the author's family. *A Single Tear* (Ningkun Wu, Atlantic Monthly Press, New York, 1993) traces the travails of a patriotic, U.S.-trained scholar who returns to China in 1950. *The Private Life of Mao Zedong: The Memoirs of Mao's Personal Physician* (Zhisui Li, with Anne Thurston, Random House, New York, 1994) combines the doctor's personal history and an intimate, controversial focus on the PRC's founding father. For a portrait of modern China, try *Behind the Wall* (Colin Thubron) and *China Wakes* (Nicholas D. Kristoff and Sheryl Wudunn, Vintage Press).

The United States and China (John K. Fairbank, Harvard University Press, Cambridge, MA, 4th ed., 1983) is a good primer on bilateral relations, while *The Great Wall and the Empty Fortress: China's Search for Security* (Andrew Nathan and Robert Ross,

Norton, New York, 1997) is a solid analysis of China's foreign policy concerns. A thoughtful collection of essays on current U.S.–China relations can be found in *Living with China: U.S.–China Relations in the Twenty-First Century* (Ezra Vogel, ed., Norton, New York, 1997). Among the scores of excellent books on Chinese politics are *Politics of China* (Roderick MacFarquhar, ed., Cambridge University Press, New York, 2nd ed., 1993) and *Sowing the Seeds of Democracy in China: Political Reform in the Deng Xiaoping Era* (Merle Goldman, Harvard University Press, Cambridge, MA, 1994).

At the juncture of politics and the economy is *China's Second Revolution: Reform After Mao* (Harry Harding, Brookings Institution, Washington, DC, 1987). *One Step Ahead in China: Guangdong Under Reform* (Ezra Vogel, Harvard University Press, Cambridge, MA, 1989) probes deeply into the changes in southern China since 1978.

One of the best windows into contemporary Chinese society is by the Chinese journalists Sang Ye and Zhang Xinxin, titled *Chinese Lives: An Oral History of Contemporary China* (ed. by W.J.F. Jenner and Delia Davin, Pantheon, New York, 1987). Western journalist Orville Schell has written several books that track China since the mid-1970s, the latest being *Mandate of Heaven: The Legacy of Tiananmen Square and the Next Generation* (Simon & Schuster, New York, 1995). *China Pop* (Jianying Jha, The New Press, New York, 1995) is a superb look at popular culture in the PRC today. *In the Red: On Contemporary Chinese Culture* (Geremie R. Barme, Columbia University Press, New York, 1999) is an important and insightful look at Chinese literature, society, and politics just before and after the Tiananmen Square massacre. For the bottom line on dissident expression—including art, culture, and politics—see *New Ghosts, Old Dreams: Chinese Rebel Voices* (Geremie Barme and Linda Jaivin, Times Books, New York, 1992).

For a taste of historical Chinese literature, spend some time with *Story of the Stone*; it's also known as *Dream of the Red Chamber*

(Xueqin Cao, trans. by David Hawkes, Penguin, New York, 1973). Any book or essay by author Lu Xun will give you a taste of China's painful path from dynastic rule through early Communist rule; try *Diary of a Madman and Other Stories* (trans. by William Lyell, University of Hawaii Press, Honolulu, 1990). *Bolshevik Salute* (Meng Wang, University of Washington Press, Seattle, 1989) is one of China's first modern novels translated into English. Of the collections of Chinese literature and poetry both ancient and modern, check out *An Anthology of Chinese Literature: Beginnings to 1911* (Stephen Owen, ed. and trans., Norton, New York, 1996) and *From May Fourth to June Fourth: Twentieth Century Chinese Fiction and Film* (David D.W. Wang and Ellen Widmer, eds., Cambridge University Press, New York, 1993).

A number of the works of Gao Xianjian, 2000 Nobel Laureate for Literature, have been translated into English. He's best known for *Soul Mountain* (HarperCollins, 2000) and *The Other Shore* (Chinese University Press, 1999). Anchee Min's best-selling *Red Azalea* (Berkley Books, New York, 1995) is a memoir of life during the Cultural Revolution. *Katherine* (Berkley Books, New York, 1996), about a young woman and her seductive American English teacher, and *Becoming Madame Mao* (Houghton Mifflin, 2000), about the powerful Jiang Ching, are other popular works of Min's. Ha Jin, who began writing by a fluke, is the author of *Waiting* (Vintage Books, New York, 2000), which won the 1999 National Book Award and the 2000 PEN/Faulkner Award for Fiction. The story tells of one man's frustration at the hands of the bureaucracy as he tries to marry the woman he loves.

VIDEOS

Among Chinese directors, Chen Kaige captures the beauty of the Chinese countryside in his mysterious, striking *Life on a String* (1991). He also directed an epic story of the artistic and personal commitment of two Peking opera stars, *Farewell, My Concubine* (1993) and *Temptress Moon* (1997). Tian Zhuangzhuang directed the controversial *The Blue Kite* (1994), a story of the

Your checklist for a perfect journey

WAY AHEAD
- Devise a trip budget.
- Write down the five things you want most from this trip. Keep this list handy before and during your trip.
- Make plane or train reservations. Book lodging and rental cars.
- Arrange for pet care.
- Check your passport. Apply for a new one if necessary.
- Photocopy important documents and store in a safe place.

A MONTH BEFORE
- Make restaurant reservations and buy theater and concert tickets. Visit fodors.com for links to local events.
- Familiarize yourself with the local language or lingo.

TWO WEEKS BEFORE
- Replenish your supply of medications.
- Create your itinerary.
- Enjoy a book or movie set in your destination to get you in the mood.

- Develop a packing list. Shop for missing essentials. Repair and launder or dry-clean your clothes.

A WEEK BEFORE
- Stop newspaper deliveries. Pay bills.
- Acquire traveler's checks.
- Stock up on film.
- Label your luggage.
- Finalize your packing list— take less than you think you need.
- Create a toiletries kit filled with travel-size essentials.
- Get lots of sleep. Don't get sick before your trip.

A DAY BEFORE
- Drink plenty of water.
- Check your travel documents.
- Get packing!

DURING YOUR TRIP
- Keep a journal/scrapbook.
- Spend time with locals.
- Take time to explore. Don't plan too much.

travails of a young schoolteacher under communism in the 1950s and '60s. (It is currently not allowed to be shown in China). The outstanding films of director Zhang Yimou, such as *Red Sorghum* (1987), *Ju-Dou* (1990), *Raise the Red Lantern* (1991), *Shanghai Triad* (1995), *The Story of Qiu Ju* (1992), and *To Live* (1994) all star the excellent actress Gong Li, whose roles range from a glamorous mob mistress in 1930s Shanghai to a rural worker.

Any film by Ang Lee is a sure delight. He was feted for his 2001 *Crouching Tiger, Hidden Dragon*, which won four Academy Awards. Lee's earlier films are also worth seeing; *Eat Drink Man Woman* and *The Wedding Banquet* are amusing looks into modern-day Chinese relationships. An American filmmaker of Chinese descent, Peter Wang, looks wryly at contemporary China in *A Great Wall* (1986).

A Western take on Chinese history is presented in Bernardo Bertolucci's *The Last Emperor*, filmed in China. Three documentary films by Ambrica Productions (New York), *China in Revolution 1911–1949* (1989), *The Mao Years 1949–1976* (1994), and *Born under the Red Flag 1976–1997* (1997), depict the political and social upheavals that followed the death of the last emperor. They are available from Zeitgeist Films (tel. 800/255–9424). The Long Bow Group (Boston) has produced *The Gate of Heavenly Peace* (1996), a documentary film about the Tiananmen Square protests; it is available from Naata (tel. 415/552–9550).

QUICK TOURS

TOUR ONE
Start with a trip to Yuyuan (Yu Garden), sip some tea, and take a walk around the surrounding old Chinese city and its old antiques markets. Afterward, work your way over to Wai Tan (the Bund) for a leisurely stroll, take a quick look at the historic Heping Fandian (Peace Hotel), and walk down Nanjing Lu to

experience Shanghai's busiest street. For dinner the Peace Hotel Chinese restaurant offers good views of the river and the Bund lighted up at night.

TOUR TWO

Take a cab north to Yufo Si (Jade Buddha Temple), head back to Nanjing Lu, and then spend an afternoon at Renmin Guang Chang (People's Square), people-watching, taking in China's ancient treasures at Shanghai Bowuguan (Shanghai Museum), and swinging over to the nearby Hua Niao Shichang (Bird and Flower Market). After dinner, catch a show of the Shanghai acrobats or relax on a night cruise of the Huangpu River.

TOUR THREE

If you have a few days in Shanghai, go beyond the city with a day trip to Zhou Zhang or Suzhou. Come back to the city for dinner in Pudong and kick off the night with a drink at one of the area's hotel bars.

In This Chapter

Updated by Paul Davidson

here and there

SHANGHAI AS A WHOLE encompasses a huge area. However, the city center is a relatively small district in what is collectively called Puxi (west of the river). On the east side lies what many think is Shanghai's future—Pudong (east of the river). Shanghai's main east–west roads are named for Chinese cities, while some north–south streets are named for Chinese provinces.

The city was once delineated by its foreign concessions, and to some extent, the former borders still define the city. The old Chinese city is now surrounded by the Zhonghua Lu–Renmin Lu circle. North of the city, the International Settlement—run by the British, Americans, Europeans, and Japanese—was the area between the Huangpu River and Huashan Lu, and bordered by Suzhou Creek to the north and Yanan Lu to the south. The former French Concession lies south of Yanan Lu, north of Zhaojiabang Lu. The southwest corner of the Concession lies at Xujiahui, from which point it runs all the way east to the Bund, with the exception of the northern half of the old Chinese city.

Although technically most Shanghainese consider the city center to be whatever lies within the Ring Road, the heart of the city is found on its chief east–west streets—Nanjing Lu, Huaihai Lu, and Yanan Lu—cut off in the west approximately at Wulumuqi Lu and in the east by the Bund. At one time, the closer you got to the Bund, the stronger the heartbeat became, but with the city's constant construction, demographics are also changing, and the heart of Shanghai seems to beat ever outward.

To the east and west of city center lie Shanghai's new development areas. In Hongqiao, the area outside the Ring Road to the west, are office and commercial buildings for foreign and domestic business and the residential area of Gubei. Rising from countryside across the Huangpu River to the east is Pudong, the new concrete behemoth that Deng Xiaoping designated as China's future financial, economic, and commercial center.

Shanghai is very much a walking city, so parts of it are easily explored on foot, and taxis are readily available. In compact central Shanghai, cab rides would be short if not for the outrageous traffic. Some spots outside Shanghai offer getaways from the city's urban chaos, and with ever-improving roads and public transportation, day trips to Suzhou and Hangzhou are possible.

Numbers in the text correspond to numbers in the margin and on the Shanghai map.

THE OLD CITY AND THE BUND

When Shanghai was carved up by foreign powers, one part of the central city remained under Chinese law and administration. These old winding back alleys eventually became notorious as a gangster- and opium-filled slum. Today the narrow meandering lanes, crowded but quaint neighborhoods, and tiny pre-1949 houses are still standing (though the vices have disappeared for the most part). A walk through the Old City gives an idea of how most Shanghainese once lived and many still do. The city's most important sightseeing spot, the Bund, on Shanghai's waterfront, showcases outstanding foreign buildings from pre-1949 times.

A Good Walk

Start at the **YUYUAN** ① (Yu Garden). Stroll through the garden, check out the bazaar surrounding it, and stop at the teahouse for a serene rest. You can also wander the small alleys of the Old City, which lies inside the Renmin Lu–Zhonghua Lu circle.

Within these alleys is a bustle of activity. Meander through the
FUYOU LU GUDAI CHANG ② (Fuyou Lu Antiques Market), or
even go farther west to the **DONGTAI LU GUDAI CHANG** ③
(Dongtai Lu Antiques Market); check out the wet market on tiny
Dajing Lu, stop in at the **CHEN XIANG GE TEMPLE** ④; or see the
only remaining piece still standing of the Old City wall at
DAJING GE ⑤.

From the Old City you can walk or take a taxi or pedicab to the
WAI TAN ⑥ (the Bund), which begins along the river. A raised
concrete promenade borders the side of the street nearest the
river. Walk north and mingle with the crowds of strolling
families, lovers walking hand in hand and camera-snapping
tourists. Continue to the intersection of Zhongshan Donglu and
Jinling Lu, marked by a triangular commercial building on the
water. If you're feeling adventurous, you can jump on a boat and
start a tour of Pudong here. The Huangpu River Cruises dock is
also nearby.

If you continue walking north, historic buildings begin
appearing on the west side of the street facing the river. Just
north of Yanan Donglu is the former **SHANGHAI CLUB** ⑦.
Farther along is the **PUDONG FAZHAN YINHANG** (the former
Hongkong & Shanghai Bank) ⑧ and the **HAIGUAN LOU** ⑨
(Customs House), which houses the Big Ching, or clock tower.
At Shanghai's main thoroughfare, Nanjing Lu, you'll see one of
the city's most famous monuments: the **HEPING FANDIAN** ⑩
(Peace Hotel) consists of the two buildings on the corner of the
Bund and Nanjing Lu. Just north of the Peace Hotel is the
ZHONGGUO YINHANG ⑪ (Bank of China), the main bank in
the city. You can spot it by all the black-market money changers
loitering in front.

Across the street on the river lies **HUANGPU GONGYUAN** ⑫
(Huangpu Park), which has a statue of Chen Yi, Shanghai's first
mayor after 1949. North of him is the obelisklike Memorial of the
Heroes of the People. At this point you've come to the junction

of the Bund and Beijing Donglu. Across the old Waibaidu Bridge on Suzhou Creek there are more pre-1949 buildings: the art deco Shanghai Dasha (Shanghai Mansions) is in front of you to the left, and the former Shanghai Stock Exchange and the Russian Consulate are to the right.

All these old buildings face the modern skyline of Pudong, which lies on the other side of the river, with the **Oriental Pearl Tower** and the **Jinmao Tower** rising above the water. The Bund provides a good vantage point for viewing both prerevolutionary and postopening and -reform Shanghai.

TIMING

It can take about two hours to stroll casually without stopping at any sights. Allow another two hours to wander through the Yuyuan Gardens, bazaar, and teahouse. Access to some of the Bund's old buildings is not allowed, but if you go inside the ones that are open to visitors, you should allow 15 minutes per building. For a cruise on the Huangpu River, count on one to three hours.

Yuyuan is almost always crowded but especially so on weekends and holidays. Shanghai's other popular tourist sights, including the Bund, are thronged with people on the weekends, but aren't too bad on weekdays.

On National Day, October 1, and Labor Day, May 1, the Bund is closed to bicycle and automobile traffic, and the roads are choked with people. On those days a fireworks show is usually put on over the water.

Sights to See

 CHEN XIANG GE TEMPLE. If you find yourself passing by this tiny temple on your exploration of the Old City, you can make an offering to Buddha with the free incense sticks that accompany your admission. Built in 1600 by the same man who built Yuyuan, it was destroyed during the Cultural Revolution and rebuilt in the 1990s. *29 Chenxiangge Lu, tel. 021/6320–3431. Y4. Daily 7–4.*

⑤ DAJING GE (Old City Wall at Dajing Road). The Old City used to be completely surrounded by a wall, built in 1553 as a defense against Japanese pirates. Most of it was torn down in 1912, except for one 50-yard-long piece that still stands at Dajing Lu and Renmin Lu. You can walk through the remnant and check out the rather simple museum nearby, which is dedicated to the history of the old city (the captions are only in Chinese). Stroll through the tiny neighboring alley of Dajing Lu for a lively panorama of crowded market life in the Old City. *269 Dajing Lu, at Renmin Lu, tel. 021/6385–2443. Y2. Tues.–Sun. 9–4.*

③ DONGTAI LU GUDAI CHANG (Dongtai Road Antiques Market). A few blocks west of the Old City, antiques dealers's stalls line the street. You'll find porcelain, Victrolas, jade, and anything else worth hawking or buying. Prices have shot up in the last few years, and fakes abound, so be careful what you buy. *Off Xizang Lu. Daily 9 AM–dusk.*

② FUYOU LU GUDAI CHANG (Fuyou Road Antiques Market). When this well-known antiques market moved from the quaint alleys of the Old City to a nondescript warehouse, it lost some of its charm. Since then, however, hawkers have started setting up their wares outside the warehouse, and some of the hustle and bustle has returned. You'll find everything from old Mao paraphernalia to old Shanghai wicker baskets to real and fake antique porcelain. Back at Fuyou Lu, some antiques stores still line the narrow lane. *457 Fangbang Zhonglu. Daily 8–dusk.*

⑨ HAIGUAN LOU (Customs House). Built in 1927, the Customs House still serves as the customs headquarters, although now in the service of a different government. The old clock tower is now called "Big Qing" by the Shanghainese. During the Cultural Revolution, the bells were taken down and replaced by speakers blaring out Mao Zedong's theme, "The East Is Red." Today the bells are back in the tower, but they can't be heard amid the cacophony of the city. *13 The Bund (Zhongshan Dong Yi Lu).*

★ **⑩ HEPING FANDIAN** (Peace Hotel). This hotel at the corner of the Bund and Nanjing Lu is among Shanghai's most treasured old buildings. If any establishment will give you a sense of Shanghai's past, it's this one. Its high ceilings, ornate woodwork, and art deco fixtures are still intact, and the ballroom evokes old Shanghai cabarets and gala parties.

The south building was formerly the Palace Hotel. Built in 1906 by the British, it is the oldest building on the Bund. The north building, formerly the Cathay Hotel, built in 1929, is more famous historically. It was known as the private playroom of its owner, Victor Sassoon, a wealthy landowner who invested in the opium trade. The Cathay was actually part of a complete office and hotel structure collectively called Sassoon House. Victor Sassoon himself lived and entertained his guests in the green penthouse. The hotel was rated on a par with the likes of Raffles in Singapore and the Peninsula in Hong Kong. It was the place to stay in old Shanghai; Noel Coward wrote *Private Lives* here. In the evenings, the famous Peace Hotel Old Jazz Band plays in the German-style pub on the first floor. *20 Nanjing Donglu, tel. 021/6321–6888.*

NEED A
BREAK?
THE PEACE HOTEL ROOF. For a memorable view, take the middle elevators to the top floor of the north building and then climb the last two flights of stairs to the roof. There's an outdoor café, from which you can see Sassoon's former penthouse and the action on the streets and river below.

⓬ HUANGPU GONGYUAN (Huangpu Park). The local government changed what once was a lovely green garden into this uninteresting concrete park. The park's only saving grace besides the **Memorial of the Heroes of the People** obelisk—is the view it offers of both sides of the river. During colonial times Chinese could not enter the park; a sign at the entrance said, NO DOGS OR CHINESE ALLOWED. *North end of Bund, beside river, tel. 021/5308–2636.*

❽ PUDONG FAZHAN YINHANG (former Hongkong & Shanghai Bank; Pudong Development Bank). One of the Bund's most impressive buildings—some say it's the area's pièce de résistance—the domed structure was built by the British in 1921–

23, when it was the second-largest bank building in the world. After 1949 the building was turned into Communist Party offices and City Hall; now it is used by the Pudong Development Bank.

In 1997 the bank made the news when it uncovered a beautiful 1920s Italian-tile mosaic in the building's dome. In the 1950s the mosaic was deemed too extravagant for a Communist government office, so it was covered by white paint, which, ironically, protected it from being found by the Red Guards during the Cultural Revolution. It was then forgotten until the Pudong Development Bank renovated the building. If you walk into the bank, look up, and you'll see the circular mosaic in the dome—an outer circle painted with scenes of the cities where the Hongkong & Shanghai Bank had branches at the time: London, Paris, New York, Bangkok, Tokyo, Calcutta, Hong Kong, and Shanghai; a middle circle made up of the 12 signs of the zodiac; and the center painted with a large sun and Ceres, the Roman goddess of abundance. 12 The Bund (Zhongshan Dong Yi Lu), tel. 021/6329–6188. Free. Weekdays 9–4:30, weekends 9–4.

❼ SHANGHAI CLUB. Built in 1910, the Shanghai Club limited membership to wealthy British men. The first floor once contained the longest bar in the world; it has since been occupied by a fast-food chain restaurant and the rest of the building became the Dongfeng Fandian (Tung Feng Hotel). Much of the building retains its original glory: the lobby still showcases its marble floor, oak paneling, columns, barrel ceiling, and beautiful old cage elevator. You can go upstairs is the Seaman's Club, which houses the new Long Bar and is frequented by sailors passing through Shanghai's harbors. 2 The Bund (Zhongshan Dong Yi Lu).

★ ❻ WAI TAN (the Bund). Shanghai's waterfront boulevard best shows both the city's pre-1949 past and its focus on the future. The district's name is derived from the Anglo-Indian and literally means "muddy embankment." In the early 1920s the Bund became the city's foreign street: Americans, British, Japanese, French, Russians, Germans, and other Europeans built banks,

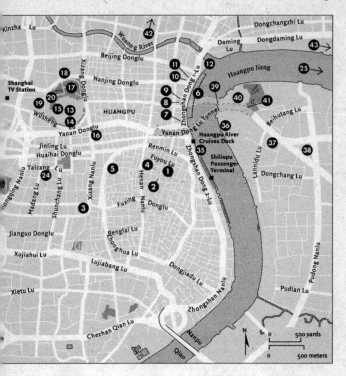

trading houses, clubs, consulates, and hotels in styles from neoclassical to art deco. As Shanghai grew to be a bustling trading center in the Yangzi Delta, the Bund's warehouses and ports became the heart of the action. With the Communist victory, the foreigners left Shanghai, and the Chinese government moved its own banks and offices here.

Today the municipal government has renovated the old buildings of this most foreign face of the city, highlighting them as tourist attractions, and even tried for a while to sell them back to the very owners it forced out after 1949.

On the riverfront side of the Bund, Shanghai's street life is in full force. The city rebuilt the promenade, making it an ideal gathering place for both tourists and residents. In the mornings just after dawn, the Bund is full of people ballroom dancing, doing aerobics, and practicing kung fu, *qi gong*, and tai chi. The rest of the day people walk the embankment, snapping photos of the Oriental Pearl Tower, the Huangpu River, and each other. In the evenings lovers come out for romantic walks amid the floodlit buildings and tower. *5 blocks of Zhongshan Dong Yi Lu between Jinling Lu and Suzhou Creek.*

★ ❶ **YUYUAN** (Yu Garden). Since the 18th century, this complex, with its traditional red walls and upturned tile roofs, has been a marketplace and social center where local residents gather, shop, and practice qi gong in the evenings. Although not as impressive as the ancient palace gardens of Beijing and accused of being overly touristed, Yu Garden is a piece of Shanghai's past, one of the few old sights left in the city.

Surrounding the garden is a touristy bazaar of stores that sell traditional Chinese arts and crafts, medicine, and souvenirs. In the last few years city renovations have turned the bazaar into a mall, complete with chrome and shiny glass—there is even a Starbucks across from the main gate to the garden. A basement antiques market with somewhat inflated prices is in the Haobao Building. On the west side of the central man-made lake is a great dumpling house famed for its xiaolong bao. You'll spot it by the long line of people outside.

To get to the garden, you must wind your way through the bazaar. The ticket booth is just north of the lake and the pleasant **Huxingting Chashi** (teahouse). The garden was commissioned by the Ming dynasty official Pan Chongtan in 1559 and built by the renowned architect, Zhang Nanyang, over 19 years. When it was finally finished it won international praise as "the best garden in southeastern China," an accolade that would be hard to defend today, especially when compared with the beautiful gardens of Suzhou. In the mid-1800s the Society of Small Swords used the garden as a gathering place for meetings. It was here that they planned their uprising with the Taiping rebels against the French colonialists. The French destroyed the garden during the first Opium War, but the area was later rebuilt and renovated.

Winding walkways and corridors bring you over stone bridges and carp-filled ponds and through bamboo forests and rock gardens. Within the park are an **old opera stage,** a **museum** dedicated to the Society of Small Swords rebellion, and the **Chenghuang Miao** (Temple of the City God). The temple was built during the early part of the Ming dynasty but was later destroyed. In 1926 the main hall was rebuilt and sometime after was renovated. The temple went through its most recent renovation in the early 1990s. One caveat: The park is almost always thronged with Chinese tour groups, especially on weekends. As with most sights in Shanghai, don't expect a tranquil time alone. *Bordered by Fuyou Lu, Jiujiaochang Lu, Fangbang Lu, and Anren Lu, Old City, tel. 021/6328–3251. Y25. Gardens, daily 8:30–5.*

....

NEED A **The HUXINGTING CHASHI** (Midlake Pavilion Teahouse; 257
BREAK? Yuyuan Lu, tel. 021/6373–6950 downstairs; 021/6373–0241 upstairs), Shanghai's oldest, opened in 1856 and stands on a small man-made lake in the middle of the Yuyuan Gardens and

Bazaar, at the center of the Bridge of the Nine Turnings. Although tea is cheaper on the first floor, be sure to sit on the top floor by a window overlooking the lake. Every night from 6:30 to 7:30 a traditional tea ceremony is performed, accompanied by three musicians playing Chinese instruments. A bottomless cup of tea comes with Chinese snacks.

⓫ **ZHONGGUO YINHANG** (Bank of China). Here, old Shanghai's Western architecture (British art deco in this case) mixes with Chinese elements. In 1937 it was designed to be the highest building in the city and surpassed the neighboring Cathay Hotel (now the Peace Hotel) by a hair, except for the green tower on the Cathay's roof. *23 Zhongshan Dong Yi Lu, tel. 021/6329–1979.*

NANJING LU AND THE CITY CENTER

The city's *zhongxin*, or center, is primarily in the Huangpu and Jingan districts. These two areas make up most of what was known in imperial and republican times as the International Settlement. Nanjing Lu, Shanghai's main thoroughfare, crosses east–west through these two districts. You can spot it at night by its neon extravaganza and in daytime by the sheer volume of business going on. Hordes of pedestrians compete with bicycles and one another, and cars move at a snaillike pace in traffic jams.

A Good Walk (or Drive)

The following long walk can also become a series of cab rides. Go west on the shopping street Nanjing Lu from the Heping Fandian, meandering among the crowds and stores. The first blocks of Nanjing Donglu are shorter and still have some of Old Shanghai's architecture. On the blocks north and south of the street you can also sense the atmosphere of the place in the 1920s. The portion of Nanjing Lu between Henan Lu and Xizang Lu is a pedestrian walkway, so no need to worry about the road's infamous traffic here. At the start of Nanjing Xilu, turn left (south) on Xizang Lu, and in a block you'll arrive at the city's huge social and cultural center, **RENMIN GUANG CHANG** ⑬, marked by an enormous TV screen on its eastern end. At the square you'll also find the wonderful **SHANGHAI BOWUGUAN** ⑭ (Shanghai Museum), the new municipal offices, and the spectacular **DA JU YUAN** ⑮ (Grand Theater). The **DA SHIJIE** ⑯ (Great World) entertainment center lies southeast of the square, on the corner of Yanan Lu and Xizang Lu.

Just north of the square is **RENMIN GONGYUAN** ⑰, Shanghai's largest and most important park, though not necessarily the nicest. On the other side of the park is the historic **GUOJI FANDIAN** ⑱ (Park Hotel).

On its western side, the People's Square is bordered by Huangpi Beilu. Turn right (north) on Huangpi Beilu, past the **HUA NIAO SHICHANG** ⑲ (Bird and Flower Market), and to your right will be the **SHANGHAI MEISHU GUAN** ⑳ (Shanghai Art Museum), at the corner of Nanjing Lu. Turn left and continue on Nanjing Lu. Once you pass Chengdu Lu, the street of the overhead Ring Road, the Shanghai Television Station and Broadcasting Building is on the left, with a very large TV screen in front. About five blocks down, after the intersection of Xikang Lu, you'll see the huge hall built by the Russians that is now the **SHANGHAI ZHANLAN ZHONGXIN** ㉑ (Shanghai Exhibition Center). It sits directly across from the convenient Shanghai Center. Two blocks farther west on Nanjing Lu, on the corner of Huashan Lu, is the **JINGAN SI** ㉒ (Jingan Temple). From here or from the Shanghai Center, jump into a cab to the important **YUFO SI** ㉓ (Jade Buddha Temple), which lies several blocks north of Nanjing Lu.

TIMING

The above walk is fairly long and doesn't have to be done all at once. You can hop a cab between sights, especially to Yufo Si. The distance from the Bund to Jingan Temple is about 4 km (2½ mi). The whole walk without stopping will probably take you 1½– 2 hours. Leave two to three hours for the Shanghai Museum. If you go to the Great World, Jingan Temple, the Bird and Flower

Market, or Yufo Si, block off an hour for each of these sights. The rest you can walk through or by very quickly.

Nanjing Lu and the People's Square are both most crowded and most exciting on weekends. You may have to fight the hordes, but you'll get a good idea of what life is like in Shanghai.

Sights to See

⑮ **DA JU YUAN** (Grand Theatre). This magnificent theater, along with the Shanghai Museum and the Shanghai Library, is part of the city's plan to remake itself as a cultural center. The theater, with its spectacular front wall of sparkling glass, has three stages, and hosts the best international and domestic performances. The dramatic curved roof atop a square base is meant to invoke the Chinese traditional saying, "The earth is square and the sky is round." See it at night. 190 *Huangpi Beilu, tel.* 021/6387–5480. *Tour* Y50. *Tours* 9–4.

⑯ **DA SHIJIE** (the Great World). A sanitized version of Old Shanghai's notorious gambling, cabaret, drug, and prostitution den has been restored. Today, the entertainment center, with its wedding cake–style tower, has turned wholesome with an eclectic set of performances—acrobatics, opera, magic, comedy, Chinese period films. Some take place in the outside courtyard. Other attractions include fortune-tellers, a Guinness Book of Records hall, fantasy rides, bumper cars, and a hall of mirrors. The center also houses fun-fair booths, a bowling alley, a dance hall, and food stalls. 1 *Xizang Nanlu, tel.* 021/6326–3760. Y25. *Daily* 9 AM–9:30 PM.

⑱ **GUOJI FANDIAN** (Park Hotel). This art deco structure overlooking People's Park was originally the tallest hotel in Shanghai. Completed in 1934, it had luxury rooms, a nightclub, and chic restaurants; today it's more subdued. 170 *Nanjing Xilu, tel.* 021/ 6327–5225.

⑲ **HUA NIAO SHICHANG** (Bird and Flower Market). At this colorful and busy market you'll find hawkers selling pets such as fish, birds, turtles, cats, and frogs; a whole range of plants, bonsai trees, orchids, and clay pots; and knickknacks and yummy snacks as well. *Huangpi Beilu between Nanjing Lu and Weihai Lu. Daily 9–dusk.*

㉒ JINGAN SI (Jingan Temple). Originally built about AD 300, the Jingan Temple has been rebuilt and renovated numerous times. The temple would be wholly forgettable were it not for its bell, which was cast in 1183. The temple is now an active Buddhist center. *1686 Nanjing Xilu, next to the Jingan Si subway entrance, tel. 021/ 6256–6366. Y5. Daily 7:30–4:45.*

⑰ RENMIN GONGYUAN (People's Park). In colonial days it was the northern half of the city's racetrack. Today the 30 acres of flower beds, lotus ponds, trees, and fairground (which is rarely open) also contain a high percentage of concrete. The park is widely known for its English corner, where locals gather to practice their language skills. *231 Nanjing Xilu, tel. 021/6327–1333. Y2. Daily 6–6.*

⑬ RENMIN GUANG CHANG (People's Square). Shanghai's main square, once the southern half of the city's racetrack, has become a social and cultural center. The Shanghai Museum, Municipal Offices, Telecommunications Building, and Grand Theater surround it. In the daytime, visitors and residents stroll, fly kites, and take their children to feed the pigeons. In the evening, kids roller-skate, people watch shows on the huge TV screen, ballroom dancers hold group lessons, and families relax together. Weekends here are especially busy. *Bordered by Weihai Lu on south, Xizang Lu on east, Huangpi Beilu on west, and Fuzhou Lu on north.*

★ ⑭ SHANGHAI BOWUGUAN (Shanghai Museum). Truly one of Shanghai's treasures, this museum has the country's premier collection of relics and artifacts. Its 11 state-of-the-art galleries house China's first exhibitions of paintings, bronzes, sculpture, ceramics, calligraphy, jade, Ming and Qing dynasty furniture, coins, seals, and art made by indigenous poplulations. The bronze collection is among the best in the world. Three additional halls house rotating exhibitions. Information is well presented in English, and the acoustic guide is also excellent. You can relax in the museum's pleasant tearoom and the excellent shops offer antiques, crafts, and reproductions of the museum's works. *201 Renmin Da Dao, tel. 021/6372–3500. Y20 (free after 4), Y60 with acoustic guide. Sun.–Fri. 9–5, Sat. 9–8.*

NEED A **ESPRESSO AMERICANO** (Shanghai Center, 1376 Nanjing Xilu, BREAK? tel. 021/6247–9750) is a nice place to get a good cup of coffee. **ESPRESSO MONICA** (Nanjing Xilu at Tongren Lu, across from Shanghai Center) is one of the few places in the city to find a real latte or cappuccino.

㉔ SHANGHAI MEISHU GUAN (Shanghai Art Museum). At the northwest corner of People's Park, the former site of the Shanghai Library was once a clubhouse for old Shanghai's sports groups, including the Shanghai Race Club. The building has become the new home of the state-run Shanghai Art Museum. There are paintings, calligraphy, and sculpture in its permanent galleries and usually modern artwork exhibitions in its other gallery. *325 Nanjing Xilu (at Huangpi Beilu), tel. 021/6327–0557. Varies, depending on exhibition. Daily 9–4.*

㉑ SHANGHAI ZHANLAN ZHONGXIN (Shanghai Exhibition Center). This mammoth piece of Russian architecture was built as a sign of Sino-Soviet friendship after 1949. Special exhibitions are held here, and the complex has a shopping area, bowling alley, and restaurant. *1000 Yanan Zhonglu, tel. 021/6279–0279. Daily 9–4.*

★ **㉓ YUFO SI** (Jade Buddha Temple). Completed in 1918, this temple is fairly new by Chinese standards. During the Cultural Revolution, in order to save the temple when the Red Guards came to destroy it, the monks pasted portraits of Mao Zedong on the outside walls so the Guards couldn't tear them down without destroying Mao's face as well. The temple is built in the style of the Song dynasty, with symmetrical halls and courtyards, upturned eaves, and bright yellow walls. The temple's great treasure is its 6½-ft-high, 455-pound seated Buddha made of white jade with a robe of precious gems, originally brought to Shanghai from Burma. Other Buddhas, statues, and frightening guardian gods of the temple populate the halls, as well as a collection of Buddhist scriptures and paintings. The 70 monks who live and work here can sometimes be seen worshiping. There's a vegetarian restaurant on the temple grounds. *170 Anyuan Lu, tel. 021/6266–3668. Y10. Daily 8–noon and 1–5.*

THE OLD FRENCH CONCESSION

The former French Concession is in the Luwan and Xuhui districts. Once populated primarily by White Russians, the area is today a charming historic district known for its atmosphere and beautiful old architecture, as well as its shopping, and bars and cafés. Most of the action centers on the main east–west thoroughfare, the tree-lined Huaihai Lu, a relaxed, upscale, international shopping street. Many of the old consulates and French buildings still line it.

A Good Walk

You can start your walk at the **ZHONGGONG YIDAHUIZHI** ㉔ (Zhongguo Gongchangdang; First Chinese Communist Party Congress site), on Xingye Lu and Huangpi Lu. From here take a cab or walk 15–20 minutes to **SUN ZHONGSHAN GUJU** ㉕ (Sun Yat-sen's Former Residence). If you walk, go south on Huangpi Lu until you reach Fuxing Lu, where you turn right. On the corner of Chongqing Nanlu and Fuxing Lu is **FUXING GONGYUAN** ㉖ (Fuxing Park). Across the way, on the southeast corner of the intersection, is a beautiful old arrowhead-shape apartment building that was once American journalist and Communist sympathizer Agnes Smedley's residence. If you continue west on Fuxing Lu, turn right at the first corner (Sinan Lu); Sun Yat-sen's Former Residence is just ahead on your right, at Xiangshan Lu. From here turn right (north), back onto Sinan Lu. At Huaihai Lu, the main street of the old French Concession, take a left. This middle stretch of the shopping street Huaihai Zhonglu is the heart of the Concession. State-run and foreign shops, boutiques, and department stores dominate the area.

Continue down a couple of blocks on Huaihai and turn right on Maoming Lu at the old **CATHAY CINEMA** ㉗. At the intersection with Changle Lu stand the historic Jinjiang and Garden hotels. On the northeast corner is the old **LYCEUM THEATRE** ㉘. If you're really into looking at old architecture, you can walk one block west and one block north to the corner of Shaanxi Nanlu and Julu Lu. Here, you can view the dollhouselike **FORMER MOLLER RESIDENCE** ㉙. Another out-of-the-way old villa complex lies farther south on Maoming Lu, at what is now the Ruijin Guest House.

Back on Huaihai Lu, continue west. After another two blocks, turn left on Fenyang Lu. The **SHANGHAI GONGYI MEISHU YANJIUSUO JIUGONG YIPIN XIUFU BU** ㉚ (Shanghai Arts and Crafts Research Institute) is in an old French mansion on this street. If you return to Huaihai Lu and continue westward, the shopping district will give way to the consulate area. You can end your walk anywhere between Fenyang Lu and Wulumuqi Lu. If you decide to continue walking, eventually you'll pass the Shanghai Library, on your left (south) side past Wulumuqi Lu. Farther down the street at the corner of Xingguo Lu is **SONG QINGLING GUJU** ㉛ (Soong Chingling's Former Residence). You can take a cab here.

Besides walking down Huaihai Lu, an excellent way of seeing the French part of town is to hop on the double-decker bus that runs up and down the thoroughfare. If you sit on the upper level, you can sneak a good view of the old homes that are otherwise hidden by compound walls.

Farther away in Xuhui District is the **XUJIAHUI DAJIAOTANG** ㉜ (Xujiahui Cathedral); from Huaihai Lu, go south on Hengshan Lu, which will end in Xujiahui. The church is on the west side of Caoxi Beilu. On the way you'll pass Shanghai's old **INTERNATIONAL CATHEDRAL** ㉝, on Hengshan Lu near Wulumuqi Lu. You'll need to take a taxi to **LONGHUA GU SI** ㉞ (Longhua Temple).

TIMING

Huaihai Lu, like Shanghai's other main thoroughfares, is most crowded on the weekends, when hordes of shoppers enjoy their weekly outings. Allow yourself at least 1–1¼ hours just to walk the above itinerary without stopping at any shops or taking a look around at the old houses. Allow about a half hour to an hour for each of the more major sights, such as Sun Yat-sen's former residence, Soong Chingling's former residence, and the site of the First National Party Congress. You can walk through some of the historic buildings, while others involve only a short look from the outside.

Sights to See

29 **FORMER MOLLER RESIDENCE.** You can't go inside, but the facade of this old Shanghai mansion, which with its colorful details and pointy roofs can only be described as part dollhouse, part castle, is the main attraction anyway. According to one myth, its tycoon owner was told by a fortune-teller that if he finished the house he would die, so he kept adding wings to ward off the Grim Reaper. Another myth says he built the house in the likeness of a mansion that his little girl once envisioned in a dream. Whatever the case, the magical building now houses the offices of the Communist Youth League. *Shaanxi Nanlu just north of Julu Lu, across from City Hotel.*

26 **FUXING GONGYUAN** (Fuxing Park). The grounds of this European-style park—known as French Park before 1949—provide a rare bit of greenery in crowded Shanghai. Here you'll find people practicing tai chi and lovers strolling hand in hand. *2 Gaolan Lu, tel. 021/6372–0662. Y1. Daily 6–6.*

33 **INTERNATIONAL CATHEDRAL.** This small ivy-covered cathedral dates to Shanghai's Concession days. Today it remains a Protestant church with regularly scheduled services. *53 Hengshan Lu, tel. 021/6437–6576.*

NEED A BREAK? The **PROMENADE** (4 Hengshan Lu) is across from the International Cathedral, in an area that has become a happening nightlife center. You'll find bars, clubs, and several restaurants. Just next door to the Promenade are the Orden Bowling Alley and Harn Sheh Teahouse.

(34) LONGHUA GU SI (Longhua Temple). Shanghai's tallest pagoda, at 131 ft, affords views of the city and surrounding countryside. The pagoda dates from the 10th century but has since been rebuilt. The temple's numerous halls have hexagonal windows, arched entryways, and roofs of curved eaves. The grounds contain a small traditional garden and a carp-filled pond. You might come upon Buddhist monks praying in the incense-filled courtyards. Attached is the Longhua Hotel and a vegetarian restaurant. *2853 Longhua Lu, tel. 021/6456–6085. Y5. Daily 7–5.*

(28) LYCEUM THEATRE. In the days of old Shanghai, the Lyceum was the home of the British Amateur Drama Club. The old stage is still in use—the theater now presents acrobatic shows. *57 Maoming Nanlu, tel. 021/6217–8530.*

NEED A BREAK? As the name **1931** (112 Maoming Nanlu, tel. 021/6472–5264) implies, this café exudes an old Shanghai atmosphere, down to the cute little tables, working Victrola and waitstaff clad in *qipao* (traditional Chinese dresses). The café serves simple drinks, coffee and tea, and excellent home-style Shanghainese cooking, with some Japanese selections, too.

One of the premier estates of old Shanghai, the **Morriss Estate**, now Ruijin Guesthouse, was built by a Western newspaper magnate. Today the estate's three huge houses, standing among green lawns and trees, have also become home to a few foreign restaurants and bars. Try the colorful restaurant/bar Zoobaa, or the Thai and Indian restaurants housed together with another bar, Face, in the north mansion, or the main mansion's lawn bar. Stroll around the estate to view its ornate details, including a stained-glass scene in the rear house.

(30) SHANGHAI GONGYI MEISHU YANJIUSUO JIUGONG YIPIN XIUFU BU (Shanghai Arts and Crafts Research Institute). It's a little dusty, run down, and bare bones, but you can watch Shanghai's artisans as they create traditional Chinese arts and crafts. Works you can purchase include everything from paper cuts and engraved chopsticks to snuff bottles and lanterns, but prices can be a bit high compared to quality. Formerly, the old French mansion housed an official of the Concession's pre-1949 government. *79 Fenyang Lu, tel. 021/6437–0509. Daily 9–5.*

③① SONG QINGLING GUJU (Soong Chingling's Former Residence). The residence from 1949 until 1963 of the wife of Dr. Sun Yat-sen has been partially preserved. The house itself is not very interesting, but the small museum next door has some nice displays from Madame Soong and Sun Yat-sen's life, including wedding pictures from their 1915 wedding in Tokyo. Madame Soong was sympathetic with the Communists, while her sister, Meiling, was married to Chiang Kai-shek. *1843 Huaihai Zhonglu, tel. 021/6431–4965. Y8. Daily 9–11 and 1–4:30.*

㉕ SUN ZHONGSHAN GUJU (Sun Yat-sen's Former Residence). Dr. Sun Yat-sen, the father of the Chinese republic, lived in this two-story house for six years, from 1919 to 1924. His wife, Soong Chingling, continued to live here after his death until 1937. Today it's been turned into a museum, and you can tour the grounds. *7 Xiangshan Lu, tel. 021/6437–2954. Y8. Daily 9–4:30.*

NEED A
BREAK? One example of Shanghai's cultural resurgence is the **YANDAN LU PEDESTRIAN STREET** (Yandan Lu between Huaihai Zhonglu and Nanchang Lu). Luwan District has repaved one block of Yandan Lu with tile, lined it with classic lampposts, thrown out all the traffic and run-down stores, and replaced them with pedestrians and quaint cafés.

㉜ XUJIAHUI DAJIAOTANG (Xujiahui Cathedral). Built by the Jesuits in 1848, this Gothic-style cathedral still holds regular masses in Chinese. *158 Puxi Lu, tel. 021/6469–0930.*

24 ZHONGGONG YIDAHUIZHI (short for Zhongguo Gongchangdang Di Yi Ci Quanguo Daibiao Dahui Huizhi Jinian Guan; Site of the First National Congress of the Communist Party of China). The secret meeting on July 31, 1921, that marked the first National Congress was held at the Bo Wen Girls' School, where 13 delegates from Marxist, communist, and socialist groups gathered from around the country. Today you can enter the house, which was renovated in 1951, and view its relics, documents, and photos. Deep in the back is the very room where the first delegates worked. It remains in its original form, complete with a table set for tea for 13 people. *374 Huangpi Nanlu, tel. 021/6328-1177. Y3. Daily 8:30-11 and 1-4.*

PUDONG NEW AREA

East of the Huangpu River lies a constantly changing urban experiment that before 1990 was farmland and rice paddies. Here now, though, is what the city and the nation hope will be the financial, economic, and commercial center of Asia. Most of the big multinationals and international banks have their Shanghai factories or headquarters here. Although much of Pudong is still empty, and its sterility can't match the pockets of charm in Puxi, it does give an idea of where Shanghai is heading. Here you'll find the biggest of everything: the tallest tower in Asia, the largest department store on the continent, and the future tallest building in the world. Among the district's wonders are the Yangpu and Nanpu bridges (supposedly the second- and third longest in the world) connecting Pudong to Puxi, the architecturally absurd International Exhibition Center, the Jinmao Tower, and of course, the Oriental Pearl Tower.

A Good Walk

You can start by crossing the Huangpu River on the **PUDONG FERRY** ㉟. Stand at the bow to get a good simultaneous view of the Bund and Pudong. The ferry drops you off at **BINGJIANG DA DAO** ㊱ (Riverside Promenade). From here you can see the most beautiful views of the Bund. Standing above Bingjiang Da Dao is the Pudong Shangri-La Hotel, where you can get a drink and a somewhat higher vantage point over the Bund.

Bear right from the Shangri-La, and you'll eventually hit Lujiazui Lu. Keep to the right (heading southeast, away from the water), and you'll be facing the skyscrapers of Lujiazui, the central financial area, or Wall Street, of Pudong. Continue walking toward the tallest high-rise in front of you, the beautiful industrial pagoda **JINMAO DASHA** ㊲. Go up to the 88th-floor observation deck for a great view, and take a sky-high break at the Grand Hyatt.

From here you can head directly east to the **SHANGHAI GUPIAO DASHA** ㊳ (Securities Exchange Building)—the building with the square hole in the middle—or back toward the water and the **DONGFANG MINGZHU** ㊵ (Oriental Pearl Tower). You'll see it towering in its gargantuan grandeur at the northwest end of Lujiazui Lu. You can take a ride to the top for yet another 360-degree view of Shanghai. The **SHANGHAI LISHI BOWUGUAN** ㊶ (Shanghai History Museum) is in the bottom of the tower.

You can walk back to the ferry terminal to return to Puxi, or you can take a trip on the **BUND TOURIST TUNNEL** ㊴, which runs underneath the Huangpu River. Other options are to jump on the subway or take a taxi across the Nanpu Bridge or through the Yanan Lu Tunnel.

TIMING

The ferry ride takes just a few minutes. You can take a leisurely stroll at Bingjiang Dadao. Then allow about 15 minutes to walk to the Jinmao from the Shangri-La and another 15 to get to the Oriental Pearl from the Jinmao, or take a short taxi ride. You can spend a half hour to an hour at the observatory decks and at the Shanghai History Museum. If lines are long, you may have to wait a while to get to the top.

Sights to See

㊱ **BINGJIANG DA DAO** (Riverside Promenade). Although the park that runs 2,750 yards along the Huangpu River is sugary-sterile in its experimental suburbia, it still offers the most beautiful views of the Bund. You can stroll the grass and concrete and view a perspective of Puxi unavailable from the west side. If you're here in the summer, you can "enjoy wading," as a sign indicates, in the chocolate-color Huangpu River from the park's wave platform. *Bingjiang Dadao. Free.*

39 BUND TOURIST TUNNEL. For a look at Shanghai kitsch at its worst, you can take a trip across the Huangpu in plastic, capsular cars. The accompanying light show is part Disney, part psychedelia, complete with flashing strobes, blowing tinsel, and swirling hallucinogenic images projected on the concrete walls. The tackiest futuristic film of the 1960s couldn't have topped this. The five-minute ride will have your head spinning and you wondering if the Chinese central government isn't giving Shanghai just a little too much money. *Entrances are on the Bund at Nanjing Donglu and in Pudong near the Riverside Promenade. Y20 one-way, Y30 round-trip.*

40 DONGFANG MINGZHU (Oriental Pearl Tower). The tallest tower in Asia (1,535 ft) has become the pride and joy of the city. It has become a symbol of the brashness and glitz of today's Shanghai. This UFO-like structure is especially kitschy at night, against the classic beauty of the Bund. Its several spheres are supposed to represent pearls (as in "Shanghai, Pearl of the Orient"). An elevator takes you to observation decks in each of the tower's four spheres. Go to the top sphere for a 360-degree bird's-eye view of the city or grab a bite in the Tower's revolving restaurant. On the bottom is the amusement center **Space City**, including laser tag and an arcade, as well as the **Shanghai History Museum**. *No. 2, Lane 504, Lujiazui Lu, Pudong, tel. 021/5879–1888. Y20, first sphere; Y100, top sphere. Daily 8 AM–9:30 PM.*

37 JINMAO DASHA (Jinmao Tower). This gorgeous 88-floor (8 being the Chinese number implying wealth and prosperity) industrial art deco pagoda is the third-tallest building in the world and the tallest in China. In it is also the highest hotel in the world—the Grand Hyatt Shanghai takes up the 53rd to 88th floors. The lower floors are taken up by office space, an entertainment center, and a neighboring exhibition center. The 88th-floor observation deck, reached in 45 seconds by two high-speed elevators, offers a 360-degree view of the city. The Jinmao, designed by Chicago's Skidmore Owings & Merrill, is both ancient and modern, Eastern and Western—the tapering tower combines the classic 13-tier Buddhist pagoda design with the postmodern steel and glass. Check out the Hyatt's dramatic 30-story atrium. *2 Shiji Dadao, tel. 021/5049–1234 Grand Hyatt. Observation deck Y50.*

⊛ PUDONG FERRY. The ferry between Pudong and Puxi, once more a necessity than a sight, is still fun to take on a nice day. The ferry labors carefully between the river's barges and boats; there are no seats, merely a lower deck entirely empty, wearily welcoming the masses. Stand at the bow for the best views of both the Pudong skyline and the Bund. *Dock on Bund at Jinling Lu, dock in Pudong at Binjiang Da Dao. Eastbound Y1, westbound free.*

⊛ SHANGHAI GUPIAO DASHA (Shanghai Securities Exchange Building). The Shanghai Stock Exchange shares its Lujiazui home with such foreign banks as the Bank of America, the Royal Bank of Canada, and the International Bank of Paris and Shanghai. The Stock Exchange Club is on the 27th floor, through which you can sometimes arrange free tours of the trading floor. *Pudong Lu north of Lujiazui Lu, tel. 021/5840–6101 Stock Exchange Club.*

⊛ SHANGHAI LISHI BOWUGUAN (Shanghai History Museum). This small museum recalls Shanghai's pre-1949 heyday with the bronze lions that once ornamented the front of the former Hongkong & Shanghai Bank building, among other curiosities. It has relocated to the building that most represents Shanghai's motley modernism—the Oriental Pearl Tower. *No. 2, Lane 504, Lujiazui Lu, Pudong, tel. 021/5879–1888. Y25. Daily 9–5*

HONGKOU DISTRICT

On the west side of the river north of Suzhou Creek are the northeastern districts of Hongkou and Yangpu. At the turn of the 20th century Shanghai was not only an international port but also an open one, where anyone could enter regardless of nationality.

As the century wore on and the world became riddled with war, Jews, first fleeing the Russian Revolution and then escaping Hitler, arrived in Shanghai from Germany, Austria, Poland, and Russia. From 1937 to 1941 Shanghai became a haven for tens of thousands of Jewish refugees. In 1943 invading Japanese troops forced all the city's Jews into the "Designated Area for Stateless Refugees" in Hongkou District, where they lived until the end of the war. Today you can still see evidence of their lives in the buildings and narrow streets of the area.

Sights to See

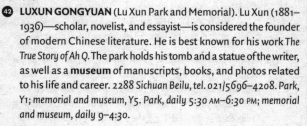

42 LUXUN GONGYUAN (Lu Xun Park and Memorial). Lu Xun (1881–1936)—scholar, novelist, and essayist—is considered the founder of modern Chinese literature. He is best known for his work *The True Story of Ah Q*. The park holds his tomb and a statue of the writer, as well as a **museum** of manuscripts, books, and photos related to his life and career. *2288 Sichuan Beilu, tel. 021/5696–4208. Park, Y1; memorial and museum, Y5. Park, daily 5:30 AM–6:30 PM; memorial and museum, daily 9–4:30.*

43 MOXI HUITANG AND HUOSHAN GONGYUAN (Ohel Moshe Synagogue and Huoshan Park). Built by Shanghai's Jewish residents in 1927, the Ohel Moshe Synagogue now has a small museum with photos and information about the Ashkenazi Jewish community of old Shanghai. Nearby Huoshan Park bears a memorial tablet erected in memory of the Jewish refugees who emigrated to the city.

Around the synagogue are lanes and old buildings that were once inhabited by Shanghai's Jewish residents. More than 20,000 Jewish refugees—engineers, lawyers, doctors, musicians, actors, writers, and academics—crowded into the district. They created their own community, with newspapers, magazines, cultural performances, and schools. Despite the crowded and unsanitary conditions, most of the Jews survived to see the end of the war, at which point the majority returned to Europe. *62 Changyang Lu, tel. 021/6512–0229.*

Beyond the City

Apart from Yuyuan and a few temples, Shanghai really doesn't have much in the way of traditional Chinese culture. However, not far from the city are several wonderful spots, which can be easily reached as day trips.

ZHOU ZHUANG. During the 12th century, Shen Wanshan, a wealthy bureaucrat, diverted the water from the Baixian River to help create this quaint, little canal town. Ramshackle houses, many of which were once mansions of the rich now occupied by peasants, line the banks, and ancient stone bridges still cross the water. The best way to tour the town is by gondola, which is relatively inexpensive and surprisingly peaceful, especially for those coming from the chaos of Shanghai. Take a minibus from Zhujia Jiao Stop to Zhou Zhuang Zhen. Kunshan Shi, Zhou Zhuang Zhen, northwest of Shanghai. *Gondola rides Y30–Y70.*

FANG TA YUAN (Square-Pagoda Garden). This relaxing, flower-filled garden is about 40 km (25 mi) outside the city center, in the small village of Songjiang (take a bus from Shanghai's main terminal to Songjiang and catch a bus to Fang ta Yuan from there). The most interesting feature of the garden is the brick wall on the north side with its depiction of a "Tan" monster. As legend has it, this creature—part deer, dragon, lion, and ox—tried to steal everything that existed in the whole world, but eventually died when he tried to swallow the sun. The view from the top floor of the pagoda is worth the seven flights of stairs. *Zhongshan Donglu, in Songjiang Village. Park admission Y5, Pagoda Y5. 6–5.*

ZUIBAI CHI (Drunken Bai's Pond). One of the nicest and most peaceful gardens around Shanghai, Zuibai Chi was built by Gu Dajia in the 17th century, who named the garden in honor of the Tang Dynasty poet, Bai Juyi (772–846). Here, Gu followed the example of the great bard, and drank inordinate amounts of alcohol while composing verse and wandering through the garden's winding corridors. *64 Renmin Nanlu, in Songjiang Village. Y5. Daily 6–5.*

In This Chapter

Updated by Paul Davidson

eating out

SHANGHAINESE FOOD IS ONE OF CHINA'S MAIN regional cuisines, like Cantonese from the south and Sichuan from the west. Shanghai's restaurants tend to serve an amalgam of dishes from different regions, and it may be difficult to weed out a restaurant that serves true Shanghainese food. Typical Shanghainese fare includes *jiachang doufu* (home-style tofu, deep-fried), *pao fou* (a soupy rice concoction), and *su ban dou* (cold vegetables with bean mash). Shanghainese chefs like to use high doses of oil and sugar and oyster sauce. River fish is often the highlight of the meal, with hairy crab a specialty in winter. Shanghai is also known for its own style of dim sum, especially *xiaolong bao* (steamed pork dumplings). You can often find dumplings, wontons, *you tiao* ("grease sticks"— deep-fried unsweetened dough), Shanghainese fried noodles, and baked and fried breads being sold by street vendors throughout the city.

Western food is now readily available, with foreign establishments arriving on the scene monthly. In addition, China's reforms have allowed fast-food joints to flourish—KFC and McDonald's are popular with locals. You often see families taking their one child for a hamburger treat or couples sharing a pizza.

Although the younger generations can be found dining or snacking into the late hours, most Chinese people follow a very strict eating schedule, so if you're dining at a more traditional Chinese restaurant, you can expect larger crowds between 11:30 AM and 12:30 PM and between 5:30 PM and 6:30 PM. At some restaurants you must arrive early for dinner (at least by 6 PM), or you'll miss all the best food. Many restaurants also have English menus, and you may find it difficult to order at the ones that don't. If you can't find a server who can translate for you, pantomime and drawings usually work fairly well.

You're not obliged to tip, as it's not a custom in China. Actually, almost all of the fancier restaurants in Shanghai tack on a 10%–15% service charge, which technically takes care of the tip even though your server may not see any of it. If there is no mandatory service charge, tipping is still not required, although more and more people are doing so at Western restaurants.

CATEGORY	COST*	
$$$$	over Y165	over US$20
$$$	Y99–Y165	US$12–$20
$$	Y50–Y99	US$6–$12
$	under Y50	under US$6

*per person for a main course at dinner

AMERICAN

$–$$ JOHNNY MOO. As its name implies, this tiny, little-known malt shop, done in a cow motif, is all about burgers. It also has great twister fries and milkshakes. *Vanke Plaza, 101, No. 5, Lane 19, Ronghua Donglu, tel. 021/6219–7589. No credit cards.*

$–$$ MALONE'S AMERICAN CAFÉ. This sports bar and grill serves American favorites such as Philly cheese steaks, buffalo wings, burgers, and pizza, as well as Asian specialties. The food isn't superb, but it's satisfying for a casual meal in a cheerful bar setting. *257 Tongren Lu, tel. 021/6247–2400. AE, DC, MC, V.*

BEIJING

$$–$$$ QUAN JU DE. Quan Ju De has been the place in Beijing to get Peking duck since 1864, but the first branch in Shanghai only opened in 1998. Expect a typical Chinese restaurant, big and noisy, complete with greasy food. The photos say U.S. president "Gorge" Bush enjoyed his duck at Quan Ju De, and you can, too. The restaurant's become so popular that a second branch has opened on Tianmu Xilu. *786 Huaihai Zhonglu, 4th fl., tel. 021/6433–7286 or 021/6433–5799. 547 Tianmu Xilu, tel. 021/6353–8558. Reservations essential.*

$–$$ **FENG ZHE LOU.** People come here for the classic setting—in the Park, one of old Shanghai's premier hotels—and for the Peking duck, which is reputedly better than any to be found in Beijing. Served with pancakes, scallions, cucumbers, and duck sauce, it can be ordered whole or by the half. The *zuixia* ("drunken shrimp"— shrimp doused in rice wine) makes a great appetizer. *170 Nanjing Xilu, tel. 021/6327–5225. Reservations essential. AE, DC, MC, V.*

BRAZILIAN

$–$$ **QUILOMBO.** Of the several Brazilian-style *churrascarias*, or barbecue restaurants, in Shanghai, this is best. The all-you-can-eat lunches and dinners come at a reasonable price, and a delicious *feijoada* (traditional Brazilian stew of pork, black beans, and rice) is served several times a week. The downstairs salsa bar offers dance lessons several times a week (admission and days vary). *41 Huaihai Zhonglu, Lane 816, tel. 021/5467–0160. AE, DC, MC, V.*

CAJUN

$$$–$$$$ **BOURBON STREET.** Not surprisingly, this is the only place in town to get Cajun and Creole food. The three-story, upscale restaurant has a relaxing patio and serves beautifully presented dishes like Louisiana crab cakes, baked oysters, shrimp creole, and jambalaya. *191 Hengshan Lu, tel. 021/6445–7556. Reservations essential. AE, DC, MC, V.*

CANTONESE

$$$–$$$$ **CANTON.** This exclusive restaurant in the Grand Hyatt serves formal Cantonese food with precision. The atmosphere is slick modernity, with an infusion of art deco. Try the soups: shark's fin or turtle. *Grand Hyatt, Jinmao Bldg., 177 Lujiazui Lu, tel. 021/5830–3338. Reservations essential. AE, DC, MC, V.*

$$$ THE DYNASTY. Although the food is mostly Cantonese, some other cuisines have entered the picture, such as the first-rate Peking duck and the Sichuan-influenced hot-and-sour soup. The Cantonese seafood dishes, especially the prawns and lobster, are particularly good. The shrimp *jiaozi* (dumplings) are delicious. *Yangtze New World Hotel, 2099 Yanan Xilu, tel. 021/6275–0000. Reservations essential. AE, DC, MC, V.*

$$ XIAN YUE HIEN. The dim sum is the big draw at Xian Yue Hien. The restaurant's Cantonese-Shanghainese menu has a healthy slant, though the amount of grease often counteracts these efforts. The original branch is nestled in Dingxiang Garden, a verdant 35-acre playground the late Qing dynasty Mandarin Li Hongzhang gave to his concubine Ding Xiang. There's outdoor seating on a large terrace, and the second floor overlooks the garden—book early if you want a table by the window. A second location recently opened on Huaihai Zhonglu. *849 Huashan Lu, tel. 021/6251–1166; 381 Huaihai Zhonglu, tel. 021/5382–2222. Reservations essential. No credit cards.*

CHAOZHOU

$$–$$$ CHAOZHOU GARDEN. This restaurant's elegant setting and excellent service complement its superb Chaozhu dishes. The core seafood offerings are creatively prepared, the poultry dishes are hearty yet virtually greaseless, and the vegetable and noodle selections are a sheer delight. The soya goose with *doufu* (tofu) appetizer is a classic Chaozhou dish. Try the crab claw with bamboo shoots and the braised shrimp and turnip casserole. Chaozhou dim sum is served during lunch. *Yangtze New World Hotel, 2099 Yanan Xilu, tel. 021/6275–0000. Reservations essential. AE, DC, MC, V.*

CHINESE

$$$ DRAGON AND PHOENIX ROOM. It's a bit touristy, and the food
★ isn't spectacular, but the atmosphere—in particular the good views of the Bund and Pudong—make the Dragon and Phoenix Room

in-the-wall—three stories, tattered and motley in decor, are dedicated to the dish. It is the place for huo guo, and there's a huge variety of produce to throw into the pot. Be forewarned: the place is so steamy that you'll leave with your clothes smelling of the spicy soup. *975 Huaihai Zhonglu, tel. 021/6415–7559. 19 Nanjing Xilu, tel. 021/6375–1590; 2118 Sichuan Beilu, tel. 021/5671–3011. No credit cards.*

$–$$ **TIANFU ZHI GUO.** The ingredients at the crowded Tianfu Zhi Guo are both plentiful and fresh. There's everything from fresh bay scallops to a local type of frog, from spinach to tofu to glass noodles to add to the concoction. *1164 Huashan Lu, tel. 021/6252–4862. Reservations essential. No credit cards.*

CHINESE VEGETARIAN

$–$$ **GONGDELIN.** Serving vegetarian specialties for more than 50 years, Gongdelin combines cuisines from all over the country in its creations. An outstanding dish is the mock duck made of tofu. Be sure to get here early; if you arrive after 6 PM, when there is always a crowd, you may not be able to get a table. *445 Nanjing Xilu, tel. 021/6327–0218. No credit cards.*

$ **ZAOZISHU.** It might be the only place in Shanghai where you can get real vegetarian food, without all the grease or imitation meats. The tofu dishes are particularly good. *77 Songshan Lu, tel. 021/5306–8001. No credit cards.*

CONTINENTAL

$$$–$$$$ **GRAND HYATT.** Two of the Grand Hyatt's restaurants present Continental cuisine while offering absolutely spectacular views of Shanghai (unless the building is shrouded in fog). The sophisticated 24-hour restaurant **Grand Café** touts its "show kitchen"—a buffet that includes appetizers, daily specials, fresh seafood, and desserts. Up on the 56th floor is the **Grill**, part of the Hyatt's three-in-one open-kitchen restaurant concept (the connecting restaurants are Japanese and Italian), where you can feast on a great seafood platter or unbelievably tender steak. *Grand Hyatt, 177 Lujiazui Lu, Pudong, tel. 021/5830–3388. Reservations essential. AE, DC, MC, V.*

$$$–$$$$ ★ **M ON THE BUND.** Espousing Shanghai's return to glamour, M does everything with flair. Exquisite Mediterranean-influenced cuisine is served in a classy and inspired chic-modern-meets-retro interior, on the top floor of a 1920s building. Start with the crepe Parmentier with caviar, and then try the baked lamb, the roasted pigeon, or the Shanghainese goose for dinner. The tables with the most envied views of the Bund are reserved for the elite, but the elegant terrace overlooking the river is great alternative, especially for brunch. *20 Guangdong Lu, tel. 021/6350–9988. Reservations essential. AE, DC, MC, V.*

$$–$$$ **50 HANKOU LU.** This restaurant is in a beautiful old British building right off the Bund. The fare is a mix of East and West, and the decor is Southeast Asian, with primitive Indonesian and New Guinean full-figure wooden sculptures. The dishes—like baked escargot, grilled steak, and Caesar salad—are artfully presented, but they're fairly rich and heavy. The restaurant offers a daily set menu at lunch (Y80–Y90) and dinner (Y180–Y200). *50 Hankou Lu, tel. 021/6329–8999 or 021/6323–8383. AE, DC, MC, V.*

$$–$$$ **LE GARÇON CHINOIS.** You'll feel like a guest in someone's home at this dimly lit restaurant in an old French villa. The walls are painted in warm hues, the art deco fittings are tasteful, and large windows frame surrounding trees and old mansions. Run by a Japanese-European couple, the restaurant presents a Continental menu: the carpaccio, grilled duck, and grilled cod fish are all sublime. For breakfast, flaky croissants and coffee are available from the café-bakery downstairs in the courtyard. *No. 3, Lane 9, Hengshan Lu, tel. 021/6431–3005 or 021/6431–1170. Reservations essential. AE, DC, MC, V.*

$$–$$$ **PARK 97.** Another sign of Shanghai's return to its decadent past, attitude is everything at this très chic establishment on the grounds

of Fuxing Park. The massive space has an art deco feel and is divided into a café, a late-night lounge, an art gallery, and a sushi bar. You can get a casual meal at the café, which serves pasta, meat dishes, and creative sandwiches and salads. At night the hip and stylish come to the lounge for a drink, while acid jazz and ambient music play in the background. *Fuxing Gongyuan, 2 Gaolan Lu, tel. 021/6318–0785. AE, DC, MC, V.*

FRENCH

\$\$\$\$ CONTINENTAL ROOM. Perched at the top of the Garden Hotel, this very elegant restaurant offers fine French food and views of the surrounding former French Concession. Chic yet traditional and extremely quiet and subdued, it's a perfect setting if you want to impress business clients. *Garden Hotel, 58 Maoming Lu, tel. 021/6415–1111. Reservations essential. AE, DC, MC, V.*

\$\$–\$\$\$ LE BOUCHON. This charming French wine bar also serves up tasty French bistro fare—crepes, quiche, salads—in a relaxed and intimate setting, with greenhouse seating for cold days and an outdoor café for when spring arrives. The main draw is the extensive selection of good and affordable wines. *1455 Wuding Xilu, tel. 021/6225–7088. Reservations essential. AE, MC, V.*

INDIAN

\$\$–\$\$\$ THE TANDOOR. Don't miss the unbelievable *murgh malai kebab*
★ (tandoori chicken marinated in cheese and yogurt mixture) or try some vegetable curries—*palak aloo* (spinach with peas) or *dal makhani* (lentil). Decorated with mirrors, Indian artwork, and Chinese characters dangling from the ceiling, the restaurant is ingeniously designed to show the route of Buddhism from India to China. The management and staff, all from India, provide impeccable service. *Jinjiang Hotel, 59 Maoming Nanlu, tel. 021/6258–2582 Ext. 9301 or 021/6472–5494. Reservations essential. AE, DC, MC, V.*

IRISH

$–$$ O'MALLEY'S. A real Irish pub, complete with the requisite superfriendly Irish staff, O'Malley's also has outdoor dining on a beautiful lawn in front of an old French mansion. The food is good and reasonably priced; the Guinness is equally good but not as kind to your wallet. *42 Taojiang Lu, tel. 021/6437–0667. AE, DC, MC, V.*

ITALIAN

$$$–$$$$ GIOVANNI'S. This upscale Italian trattoria has a good view of the Hongqiao area. The *zuppa di pesce alla Veneziana* (Venetian fish soup) is spectacular, as is the calamari, and the pastas are served perfectly al dente. Be sure to try the flat bread with aromatic olive oil—a treat in Shanghai. The crème brûlée is extraordinary. *Westin Tai Ping Yang, 27th floor, 5 Zunyi Nanlu, tel. 021/6275–8888. Reservations essential. AE, DC, MC, V.*

$$$ AD. Former head chef of Giovanni's, Antonio Donnaloia spared no expense in creating his own opera—marble, antique furniture, Gianni Versace uniforms, vaulted ceilings, a fireplace inside what looks like a plaster-of-Paris head of Zeus, and Italian fabric on the walls and furniture. With the exception of a few appetizers, the food is superb: the deep-fried calamari and prawns, the mixed seafood Amalfi soup, the hearty but delicious risotto, some of the best veal in Shanghai, and grilled portions of fresh, imported seafood. Don't miss the to-die-for desserts, such as the poached pear with cinnamon mousse and the *tartufo bianco*. *3896 Hongmei Beilu, tel. 021/6262–5620. Reservations essential. AE, DC, MC, V.*

$$$ DAVINCI'S. This chic establishment offers nouvelle Italian food. For starters, a colorful selection from the antipasto table can include carpaccio, eggplant salad, calamari, and Italian cold cuts. In addition to the excellent pastas and risotto, the meat dishes are outstanding, especially the lamb dusted with rosemary. *Shanghai Hilton, 250 Huashan Lu, tel. 021/6248–0000 Ext. 8263. Reservations essential. AE, DC, MC, V. No lunch.*

$–$$ PASTA FRESCA DA SALVATORE. The food isn't outstanding at this casual trattoria, but it's the only place to go for reasonably priced Italian food. The pizza here is better than the pasta. The set lunch menu costs Y68. *Friendship Shopping Centre, 6 Zunyi Nanlu, tel. 021/6270–4693 or 021/6270–0000 Ext. 1211; 4 Hengshan Lu, tel. 021/6473–0772. AE, DC, MC, V.*

JAPANESE

$$$$ YAMAZOTO. The owners of this restaurant (and the pretentious hotel it is located in) seem to have forgotten that they are in China and not downtown Tokyo. The food is good, the sushi is fresh, but the prices are really outrageous. However, if you have a client whom you are trying to impress, this is a good place to blow some expense-account money. *Garden Hotel, 58 Maoming Nanlu, tel. 021/6415–1111. Reservations essential. AE, DC, MC, V.*

$$$–$$$$ SHINTORI. With its characters etched in glass partitions and water and rock installations, this top-rate Japanese restaurant has chic postmodernism written all over it. The Taiwanese-owned establishment offers sublime and stylish dishes from excellent sushi to grilled cod to seafood steamed in sake. The nine-course set menu (Y395) is an experience. *288 Wulumuqi Nanlu, tel. 021/6467–1188. Reservations essential. AE, MC, V.*

$$–$$$ O-EDO (DA JIANG HU). This quaint Japanese restaurant is known for its all-you-can-eat-and-drink-for-Y200 offer. Expect an inordinate amount of sushi, sashimi, tempura, broiled cod, *agedashi* tofu, chicken yakitori, and so on—all washed down with a bottomless barrel of sake. The house specialty is the delicious raw beef *tataki* and *okoze* (stonefish). *30 Donghu Lu, tel. 021/6467–3332; 2430 Xietu Lu, tel. 021/6468–5177. No credit cards.*

$$–$$$ ITOYA. The small, unassuming Itoya serves imposing portions of some of the freshest and tastiest fish in town. The menu is filled with a variety of satisfying traditional Japanese dishes like broiled cod, tempura, and reasonable lunch boxes, but the place to head for is the sushi bar. Itoya's other claim to fame is its 60 different kinds of sake. *24 Ruijin Er Lu, tel. 021/6467–0758; Ronghua Xidao, Lane 19, No. 6, tel. 021/6219–2286; 381 Huaihai Zhonglu, 3F, tel. 021/5382–5777; 1515 Nanjing Xilu, tel. 021/5298–5777. AE, DC, MC, V.*

KOREAN

$–$$ ALILANG. One of Shanghai's oldest Korean eateries, Alilang serves kimchi (pickled cabbage), unlimited cold appetizers, meat and seafood barbecued on smoky coals right before your eyes, and noodles. The meat dishes are the best choice here, although they fall a bit short of other Korean places in town. A specialty that is always delicious is the *congyoubing* (onion cake). *28 Jiangsu Beilu, tel. 021/6252–7146. AE, DC, MC, V.*

$–$$ GAO LI KOREAN RESTAURANT. Hidden on a small lane, Gao Li is a bit of a hole in the wall, but it serves great, cheap food to crowds of diners until 2 AM, specializing in tender and delicious grilled meat. The noodle dishes are some of the best in town: try the cold vermicelli noodle appetizer. *No.1, Lane 181, Wuyuan Lu, tel. 021/6431–5236. No credit cards.*

MEXICAN

$–$$ BADLANDS. This tiny restaurant draws foreign residents for quick and cheap Mexican food and the cheerful, friendly environment, which includes an outdoor deck and a bamboo bar. The favorites here are the burritos and tacos. On weekends Badlands also serves a Tex-Mex breakfast. *897 Julu Lu, tel. 021/6466–7788 Ext. 8003. AE, DC, MC, V.*

MUSLIM/UIGHUR/MIDDLE EASTERN

$–$$$ ALI YY. Ali YY's ground-floor Xinjiang restaurant serves good, wholesome Uighur food for bargain prices. Dishes are low on grease and high on flavor. Try the fried Xinjiang noodles and the lamb kebabs. Upstairs, proprietor Kenny Tang (owner of the nightclub YY) has opened an Arabic restaurant, where he has made eating a true event, complete with superstylish soft red-velvet cushions, and your own personal pair of Ali YY slippers. Upstairs Y200 will buy you great platters of hummus and falafel. *5B Dongping Lu, tel. 021/6415–9448. Reservations essential. No credit cards.*

PORTUGUESE

$$–$$$ SANDOZ. This is Shanghai's first and only Portuguese restaurant. The chef, from Macau, cooks traditional Portuguese foods, such as *bacalhau* (codfish) and chorizo, as well as some famous Macanese dishes. Sandoz also has a great selection of wines and outdoor seating for when the weather is warm. *207 Maoming Nanlu, tel. 021/ 6466–0479. AE, DC, MC, V.*

SHANGHAINESE

$$–$$$ BIG FAN (DA FENG CHE). The wood-paneled walls of this restaurant—in a 1930s apartment village—are decorated with framed colonial advertisements and banknotes, along with photos of street scenes, garden parties, and men's clubs from the 1930s. As you're seated, a waiter will pour you Sichuan tea in the traditional style from a pot with a foot-long spout. The cooking is home-style Shanghainese, with the seafood dishes standing out. *1440 Hongqiao Lu, tel. 021/6275–9131 Ext. 268. No credit cards.*

$$–$$$ HENRY. Right in the heart of the former French Concession, Henry has a '20s retro feel, with huge French windows in the front, and jazz streaming quietly over the sound system. The atmosphere is very old Shanghai and classy, but the food—soup, noodles, lemon chicken, homestyle tofu—and service are sometimes hit or miss. *8 Xinle Lu, tel. 021/6473–3448.*

$$–$$$ 1221. This stylish but casual eatery has become a favorite of its
★ hip Chinese and expatriate regulars. Shanghainese food is the mainstay, but just about everything is on the menu. The dishes are imaginative, the service attentive, and the atmosphere pleasing. From the extensive 11-page menu (in English, pinyin, and Chinese), you can order dishes like sliced *you tiao* (fried bread sticks) with shredded beef, a whole chicken in a green-onion soy sauce,

delicious shredded pork with sweet bean sauce and small pancakes, and *shaguo shizi tou*, or "Lion's Head" meatballs. *1221 Yanan Xilu, tel. 021/6213–6585 or 021/6213–2441. Reservations essential. No credit cards.*

$–$$ GAP SALON (JINTING JIUJIA). The Gap Salon, on Maoming Lu, is a spectacle you won't soon forget. This 20,500-square-ft establishment offers its mostly Chinese clientele just about everything—food, music, dancing, karaoke—with European decor (or at least what the Hong Kong–Chinese owners perceive as European). A genuine antique Red Flag—the car exclusively used by Shanghai officials of yesteryear—overhangs the entrance, hinting at the grandiosity to come. A huge central area evokes an outdoor courtyard. Filipino bands and Chinese dancers take the stage during your meal. Four other locations offer the same hearty Shanghainese food in somewhat more mellow environments. *127 Maoming Nanlu, tel. 021/6433–9028; 8 Zunyi Lu, tel. 021/6278–2900; Westgate Mall, 1038 Nanjing Xilu, 4/F, tel. 021/6218–6868; 960 Caoxi Beilu, tel. 021/6481–3249; The Promenade, 8 Hengshan Lu, tel. 021/6473–4828. Reservations not accepted. AE, DC, MC, V.*

$–$$ LULU. This small, crowded, smoke-filled restaurant is the hip late-night place for Shanghai's young fashionable crowd. Lulu is known for its fresh seafood; you'll be able to see what you're getting in the tanks lined up inside the entrance. The shredded pork and scallion wrapped in pancakes is also perfectly executed and *kofu* (cold braised tofu) doesn't get any better than this. Sometimes it's difficult to get a table, even at 3 in the morning, so be prepared to wait, especially on weekends. The Pudong branch is similarly crowded. *336 Shuicheng Nanlu, tel. 021/6270–6679; 161 Lujiazui Lu, Pudong, tel. 021/5882–6679. Reservations essential. AE, DC, MC, V.*

SICHUANESE

$$–$$$ SICHUAN COURT. Get a sky-high view of the city at this sleek upscale eatery at the top of the Hilton. The Sichuan treasure box offers a good array of delicacies—cold sliced garlic pork, sliced suckling pig, sliced duck, some cold vegetables—to start off with. The tea-smoked duck (smoked on order in Chengdu), *mapo doufu* (spicy tofu), and *dan dan* (noodles) are typical of the Sichuan dishes served here. *250 Huashan Lu, tel. 021/6248–0000. Reservations essential. AE, DC, MC, V.*

$$ SICHUAN RESTAURANT. Here the most popular dish, which you'll see on almost every table, is the stewed beef. If you want something really spicy, typical of Sichuan food, try the crispy chicken. The restaurant also serves 14 varieties of Sichuan dim sum that come at a bargain. More daring choices such as fish maw, turtle, snake, pigeon, and frog are served up with unexpected flavors like almond bean curd, chili and peanuts, preserved eggs, and fried squid shreds with chili. *739 Dingxi Lu, tel. 021/6281–0449. AE, DC, MC, V.*

$ XIN CHONGQING. This place is *hot* in the true Sichuan sense of the word—it's the local hangout for diehard chili fans. Try the *lazi ji* (chili chicken), *douhua* (tofu pudding), and the *nangua bing* (pumpkin cakes). The menu is in Chinese only, however, and there are no pictures to aid those who are not familiar with the language. *98 Puhui Tang Lu, tel. 021/6428–6236. No credit cards.*

SINGAPOREAN

$–$$ ★ FRANKIE'S. The bare decor and a-bit-too-bright lighting don't discourage connoisseurs of Singaporean cuisine. The fried *kway teow* (an absolutely delicious version of the Singaporean noodle dish), the chicken curry, and the stir-fried broccoli with garlic are especially good, but the standout dish is the pepper crab. Don't miss the refreshing dessert made with coconut milk. *118 Changde Lu, tel. 021/6247–0886. No credit cards.*

TAIWANESE

$–$$ XIAO MUWU. When the weather's warm and it's not raining, this bamboo restaurant becomes an open-air eatery reminiscent of

Thailand. The specialty of the house is barbecued meat and seafood marinated in Taiwanese hot spices. You order by the piece, and the chef cooks it on the spot. The best items are the barbecued squid, chicken, and tofu. *825 Zhaojiabang Lu, tel. 021/6428–1402; 665 Shenxia Lu, tel. 021/6273–9337; 618 Beijing Xilu, tel. 021/6218–8078. No credit cards.*

THAI

$$–$$$ **IRENE'S.** The Judy's Group, responsible for the nightclub Judy's Too, designed this restaurant to look like a traditional teahouse complete with a few low tables and cushions on the floor, colorful Thai textiles, and wooden statues. The Thai food is good if not inspired, though the salads—especially the papaya salad—are wonderful. There is an all-you-can-eat buffet, with drinks included, every day except Saturday. *263 Tongren Lu, tel. 021/6247–3579. Reservations essential. AE, DC, MC, V.*

In This Chapter

Updated by Paul Davidson

shopping

BECAUSE OF SHANGHAI'S COMMERCIAL STATUS as China's most open port city, it has the widest variety of goods to be found in the nation, with the exception of Hong Kong. Ritzy chrome shopping malls stand alongside the local dingy state-run stores, inundating the consumer with both foreign name brands and domestic goods. Two of Shanghai's main roads, Nanjing Lu and Huaihai Lu, have become the city's shopping meccas.

Traditional treasures, Chinese arts and crafts, and such special exports as silk and linen are available in stores as well as on the street. In the city's nooks and crannies, outdoor markets give a good view of Shanghai's bustling street life. Food markets are scattered in every neighborhood. Bird and flower markets offer everything from bonsai plants to songbirds. Most interesting, however, are the antiques markets, at which local hawkers sell their pieces of Chinese history—some real, some not.

ANTIQUES AND FURNITURE

Antiques markets, shops, and furniture warehouses abound in Shanghai, as increasing numbers of foreigners, lured by news of great deals, flock to the city. Great deals, however, are gradually becoming only good deals. No matter what or where you buy, bargaining is an inescapable part of the sales ritual. Note that fake antiques are often hidden among real treasures. Also be aware of age: The majority of pieces date from the late Qing (1644–1911) dynasty; technically, only items dated after 1797 can be legally exported. When buying antique furniture, it helps to know age, of course, and also what kind of wood was used.

Although the most commonly used was elm, a whole variety of wood can be found in Chinese antiques. All shops will renovate any pieces you buy.

The daily **DONGTAI LU MARKET** (Off Xizang Lu) offers goods in outside stalls lining the street. The **FUYOU LU** (457 Fangbang Zhonghu) Sunday market in the Old City, now open daily since it moved off the streets into a nondescript warehouse, still bustles as hawkers set up their goods in front of the warehouse. The **HAOBAO BUILDING** (Yuyuan Garden, 265 Fangbang Lu, tel. 021/6355–9999) houses a basement floor with 250 booths selling antiques. The government-owned **SHANGHAI ANTIQUE AND CURIO STORE** (218–226 Guangdong Lu, tel. 021/6321–4697) has some good pieces; there's no bargaining, but you're sure not to get a fake, and the receipts are official.

Some **WAREHOUSES** to try are at 307 Shunchang Lu (tel. 021/6320–3812) and 1430 Hongqiao Lu and 1970 Hongqiao Lu, (tel. 021/6242–8734). The **LI BROTHERS** (1220 Hongmei Lu, tel. 021/6436–1500 Ext. 195) run an antiques warehouse.

ARTS AND CRAFTS

Shanghai's artisans create pieces of traditional Chinese arts and crafts right before your eyes at the **ARTS AND CRAFTS RESEARCH INSTITUTE** (79 Fenyang Lu, tel. 021/6437–0509), where you can purchase everything from paper cuts to snuff bottles, from lanterns to engraved chopsticks. The state-owned **FRIENDSHIP STORE** (40 Beijing Donglu, tel. 021/6329–4600)— a chain for foreigners that started in major Chinese cities as a sign of friendship when China first opened to the outside world—has evolved into a six-story department store selling foreign and domestic goods; it welcomes everyone. It's touristy but a good quick source of Chinese arts and crafts (snuff bottles, jewelry, calligraphy, fans, vases, jade, lanterns, etc.) and silk. The state-owned **SHANGHAI JINGDEZHEN PORCELAIN STORE**

(1175 Nanjing Xilu, tel. 021/6253–3178) has a large selection of porcelain ware and other arts and crafts.

CARPETS

Beijing has always been a better place to buy Chinese rugs, but Shanghai has a few shops that may give you a good deal. The **CARPET FACTORY** (783 Honggu Lu, tel. 021/6327–6539) has a wide selection of rugs. The **SHANGHAI ARTS AND CRAFTS TRADING COMPANY** (Shanghai Exhibition Centre, 1000 Yanan Xilu, tel. 021/6279–0279 Ext. 62222) has carpets as well as other handcrafts. You can watch artisans weave the carpets at **SHANGHAI PINE AND CRANE CARPET STORE** (410 Wukang Lu, tel. 021/6431–7717). You can take a tour of the **ZHAOHU CARPET FACTORY** (98 Gubei Nanlu, tel. 021/6436–1713) before you decide to buy.

CHINESE MEDICINE

For Chinese medicines, try **CAITONGDE DRUGSTORE** (320 Nanjing Donglu, tel. 021/6350–4740). There are traditional cures and health products at **JINSONG GINSENG AND DRUG STORE** (823 Huaihai Zhonglu, tel. 021/6437–6700). For a selection of traditional as well as Western medicines, go to **SHANGHAI NO. 1 DISPENSARY** (616 Nanjing Donglu, tel. 021/6473–9149).

DAILY NECESSITIES

Shanghai's modern supermarkets should be able to supply you with most personal-use and food products. **WATSON'S DRUG STORES** (Shanghai Center, 1376 Nanjing Xilu, tel. 021/6279–8381; 789 Huaihai Zhonglu, tel. 021/6474–4775) is the most reliable pharmacy. **THE MARKET** (Shanghai Center, 1376 Nanjing Xilu) can be counted on for products you can't find anywhere else in the city.

Beyond T-Shirts and Key Chains

You can't go wrong with baseball caps, refrigerator magnets, beer mugs, sweatshirts, T-shirts, key chains, and other local logo merchandise. You won't go broke buying these items, either.

BUDGET FOR A MAJOR PURCHASE If souvenirs are all about keeping the memories alive in the long haul, plan ahead to shop for something really special—a work of art, a rug or something else hand-crafted, or a major accessory for your home. One major purchase will stay with you far longer than a dozen tourist trinkets, and you'll have all the wonderful memories associated with shopping for it besides.

ADD TO YOUR COLLECTION Whether antiques, used books, salt and pepper shakers, or ceramic frogs are your thing, start looking in the first day or two. Chances are you'll want to scout around and then go back to some of the first shops you visited before you hand over your credit card.

GET GUARANTEES IN WRITING Is the vendor making promises? Ask him to put them in writing.

ANTICIPATE A SHOPPING SPREE If you think you might buy breakables, include a length of bubble wrap. Pack a large tote bag in your suitcase in case you need extra space. Don't fill your suitcase to bursting before you leave home. Or include some old clothing that you can leave behind to make room for new acquisitions.

KNOW BEFORE YOU GO Study prices at home on items you might consider buying while you're away. Otherwise you won't recognize a bargain when you see one.

PLASTIC, PLEASE Especially if your purchase is pricey and you're looking for authenticity, it's always smart to pay with a credit card. If a problem arises later on and the merchant can't or won't resolve it, the credit-card company may help you out.

FABRICS AND TAILORS

For silk clothing, the **FRIENDSHIP STORE** (40 Beijing Donglu, tel. 021/6329–4600) has a good selection. The **GOLDEN DRAGON SILK AND WOOL COMPANY** (816 Huaihai Zhonglu, tel. 021/6473–6691) has the best fabric selection in town. The **JINLING SILK COMPANY** (363 Jinling Donglu, tel. 021/6320–1449) has a wide choice. The **SHANGHAI SILK COMMERCIAL COMPANY** (139 Tianping Lu, tel. 021/6282– 5021) offers good quality.

Shanghai is home to many tailors who make clothing at reasonable prices. The most inexpensive are to be found at **TAILOR LANE,** a small alley leading to Hunan Lodge on Wuyuan Lu (Nos. 52 and 72) near Maison Mode; bring in a garment to copy. **ASCOT CHANG** (Dickson Center, 400 Chang Le Lu, Room 211, tel. 021/6472–6888) makes quality suits, shirts, and other clothing. **SAKURAI YOFUKU** (Friendship Shopping Center, 6 Zunyi Lu, tel. 021/6270–0000) produces good clothing. The jovial and most reasonably priced **TAYLOR LEE** (2018 Huaihai Lu) specializes in men's and women's suits.

A few tailors specialize in making Chinese *qipaos* (cheongsams). The one at 258 Shimen Yi Lu does good work, as does the cute Shanghai Tang–like store on the west side of Maoming Lu south of Nanchang Lu. There are more cheongsam stores in a row on the south side of Changle Lu between Shaanxi Lu and Maoming Lu. **LONG FENG** (942 Nanjing Xilu) makes cheongsams.

OUTDOOR MARKETS

Most of Shanghai's outdoor markets sell food and produce. The **BIRD AND FLOWER MARKET** (Huangpi Lu between Nanjing Lu and Weihai Lu) gives a good slice of Shanghai life: you'll find hawkers selling pets such as fish, birds, turtles, cats, and frogs, and a whole range of plants, bonsai trees, orchids, and clay pots. You can find good, cheap Western clothing—seconds, irregulars, and knockoffs—at **HUATING MARKET** (Huating Lu between Changle Lu and Huaihai Zhonglu). The biggest market in

Shanghai is the **ZHONGHUA XIN LU MARKET** (100 Hengfeng Lu), which attracts private hawkers who sell everything under the sun.

TEA

The **SHANGHAI HUANGSHAN TEA COMPANY** (853 Huaihai Zhonglu, tel. 021/6545–4919), with nine shops around Shanghai, sells a huge selection of China's best teas by weight; the higher the price, the better the tea. Beautiful Yixing pots are also for sale.

WESTERN-STYLE DEPARTMENT STORES AND MALLS

In Shanghai, there are very few typical malls in the Western sense. At Isetan and the Orient, which are in large, department-store-like buildings, different brands are featured in different spaces. These places are organized like department stores, but the occupants are not all employed by one company. The 10-story **BABAIBAN DEPARTMENT STORE** (501 Zhangyang Lu, Pudong, tel. 021/5830–1111) sells it all—clothes, household goods, shoes, accessories, cosmetics, sporting goods, arts and crafts, exercise equipment, stationery, audio/visual equipment, office equipment, even cars.

The large, state-run **HONGQIAO FRIENDSHIP SHOPPING CENTRE** (6 Zunyi Lu, tel. 021/6270–0000) has everything, including Western finesse in merchandising—household items, gifts, cosmetics, clothing, furniture and audio/video equipment, and a grocery store and deli. The Japanese-run **ISETAN** (527 Huaihai Zhonglu, tel. 021/6375–1111; Westgate Mall, 1038 Nanjing Xilu, tel. 021/6218–7878), one of the most fashionable in Shanghai, carries such brands as Lancôme, Clinique, Benetton, Esprit, and Episode.

The **ORIENT SHOPPING CENTER** (8 Caoxi Beilu, tel. 021/6407–1947) is the biggest and most comprehensive of three major department stores in Xujiahui. **PRINTEMPS** (939–947 Huaihai Zhonglu, tel. 021/6431–0118), the leader in French department stores, opened a beautiful branch, designed in the same style as the 130-year-old Printemps in Paris, in the center of Shanghai's old French Concession; most goods sold are at a price far too high for the ordinary Chinese person.

The famous **SHANGHAI NO. 1 DEPARTMENT STORE** (830 Nanjing Donglu, tel. 021/6322– 3344) is Shanghai's largest state-owned store and attracts masses of Chinese shoppers, especially on weekends; its seven floors have an amazing plethora of domestic items. **WESTGATE MALL** (1039 Nanjing Xilu, tel. 021/6218–6868) is a genuine mall in the Western sense.

In This Chapter

Updated by Paul Davidson

outdoor activities and sports

CHINA DOESN'T SHARE JAPAN'S ENTHUSIASM for Western sports, but professional basketball has had some moderate success in Shanghai and there are more than a few options for golf right outside the city. Unless you know tai chi, your best bet for personal fitness is at an indoor health club at a Western hotel. Better yet, rent a bicycle and cruise down the tree-shaded bike lanes.

PARTICIPANT SPORTS

Golf

All clubs and driving ranges run on a membership basis, but most allow nonmembers to play when accompanied by a member. Some even welcome the public. Most clubs are outside the city, in the suburbs and outlying counties of Shanghai.

GRAND SHANGHAI INTERNATIONAL GOLF AND COUNTRY CLUB (Zhengyi Town, Kunshan City, Jiangsu Province 215347, tel. 021/6210–3350) is an 18-hole championship course and driving range. **SHANGHAI DIANSHAN LAKE GOLF CLUB** (Jiang Su, Kun Shan Shi, Ding Shan Hu Zen, tel. 0520/748–1111), a 27-hole course on Dianshan Lake designed by Bobby J. Martin, includes a driving range. **SHANGHAI EAST ASIA GOLF CLUB** (135 Jianguo Xilu, tel. 021/6433–1351) has a driving range. **SHANGHAI INTERNATIONAL GOLF AND COUNTRY CLUB** (Zhu Jia Jiao, Qingpu County, tel. 021/5972–8111), an 18-hole course, has a driving range and a three-hole practice course.

SHANGHAI LINKS GOLF AND COUNTRY CLUB (Tianxu Township, San Jia Bay, Pudong, tel. 021/5882–2700), a Jack Nicklaus Signature–designed course, has nine holes so far. **SHANGHAI RIVIERA GOLF RESORT** (Xiang Er, Nanxiang, Jiading County, tel. 021/5912–8836) is an 18-hole course and driving range. **SUN ISLAND INTERNATIONAL CLUB** (Sun Island, Shenxiang, Qingpu County, tel. 021/5983–0888), an 18-hole course designed by Nelson Wright Haworth, also has a driving range. **TOMSON PUDONG GOLF CLUB** (1 Longdong Lu, Pudong, tel. 021/5833–9999) is an 18-hole course with a driving range, designed by Shunsuke Kato.

Health Clubs, Swimming Pools, and Tennis Courts

Most of the best health clubs, gyms, and pools are at the Western hotels. Fees are charged for those who are not hotel guests. The **GARDEN HOTEL** (58 Maoming Nanlu, tel. 021/6415–1111) has an Olympic-size indoor pool. **HOLIDAY INN CROWNE PLAZA** (400 Panyu Lu, tel. 021/6280–8888) has tennis and squash courts. The **KERRY CENTER** (1515 Nanjing Xilu, tel. 021/6279–4625) has aerobics and weight rooms and a swimming pool.

The **PORTMAN RITZ-CARLTON** (1376 Nanjing Xilu, tel. 021/6279–8888) has a swimming pool and comprehensive aerobics and weight rooms, as well as tennis, squash, and racquetball courts. If you're not a hotel guest or a member, you can enter only with a member, at a fee of Y100. The impressive sports center and gym at the **REGAL INTERNATIONAL EAST ASIA HOTEL** (516 Hengshan Lu, tel. 021/6415–5588) has world-class tennis courts, a 25-meter indoor pool, squash courts, an aerobics room, a simulated golf-driving range, and a 12-lane bowling alley.

The **SHANGHAI HILTON** (250 Huashan Lu, tel. 021/6248–0000) has a good health club. If you're looking for an outdoor pool, you can find a beautiful one at the **SHANGHAI INTERNATIONAL CONVENTION HOTEL** (2106 Hongqiao Lu, tel. 021/6270–3388). The **SHANGHAI JC MANDARIN** (1225 Nanjing Xilu, tel. 021/6279–1888) has good tennis and squash courts. Some of the city's best tennis courts can be found at the **XIJIAO GUEST HOUSE** (1921 Hongqiao Lu, tel. 021/6433–6643).

Outside the hotels, the American chain **GOLD'S GYM** (288 Tongren Lu, tel. 021/6279–2000) has arrived in Shanghai, with comprehensive fitness classes and weight rooms, open 24 hours a day.

Yachting

Shanghai isn't known for its boating, but if you go out to Dianshan Lake, you can enjoy water sports in style at the **REGENCY INTERNATIONAL YACHT CLUB** (1860 Hongqiao Lu, tel. 021/6242–3632), an elite, members-only club (that admits nonmembers for a fee) with a clubhouse, a pool, and food and beverage outlets. It provides boats, sailboats, jet skis, kayaks, surfboards, water skis, parasailing, and overnight accommodations in cabins right on the lake.

SPECTATOR SPORTS

Professional league basketball is growing increasingly popular in Shanghai, with foreign-sponsored teams that include American professional players. The Hilton Basketball League plays an annual season from November through April at the **LUWAN GYMNASIUM** (128 Jiaozhabang Lu; tel. 021/6427–8673 IMG Sports Management). Games are occasionally played at the **SHANGHAI GYMNASIUM** (1111 Caoxi Beilu, tel. 021/6473–0940).

The overwhelmingly grandiose, UFO-like **SHANGHAI STADIUM** (666-800 Tianyaoqiao Lu, tel. 021/6426–6888 Ext. 8268) seats 80,000 spectators and holds athletic events regularly, especially soccer matches.

In This Chapter

Updated by Paul Davidson

nightlife and the arts

OTHER CITIES IN CHINA CLOSE DOWN after dinner, but Shanghai never sleeps. Whether playing pool at an American bar or dancing the night away at a chic club, young Shanghainese and expatriates alike have a fairly good selection of nighttime entertainment.

Most of the city's popular bars are in the center, concentrated in areas of the Luwan, Xuhui, and Jingan districts. And because Shanghai is small and traffic is light in the evenings, it's easy to bar-hop by cab. Karaoke is ubiquitous; KTV (Karaoke TV) establishments with private rooms complete with hostesses, XO cognac, and fruit platters are even more popular. Just beware of the prices.

For up-to-date information about what's going on in the city, check out *Shanghai Talk* and *That's Shanghai*, the monthly expatriate magazines available at Western bars, restaurants, and hotels throughout town; the *Shanghai Star*, the English-language newspaper published by the *China Daily*; or *Shanghai Now*, available at most hotels and bookstores.

NIGHTLIFE

Bars

The **COTTON CLUB** (1428 Huaihai Zhonglu, tel. 021/6437–7110), a comfortable, unassuming, and relaxed lounge, is the place for live music, with blues and jazz by Chinese and foreign musicians. The historic and romantic **PEACE HOTEL** (20 Nanjing Donglu, tel. 021/6321–6888) has a German-style pub that has gained fame due to the nightly performances (Y50–Y80, depending on where you sit) of the Peace Hotel Old Jazz Band, whose members played jazz in dance halls in pre-1949 Shanghai.

If you're looking for the trendy, young Chinese hipsters and the more alternative local crowds, check out the Shanghai–cum–New York establishments. The minimalist **BONNE SANTE** (Regency Shanghai, 8 Jinan Lu, tel. 021/6384–2906) reads like a monochrome Manhattan apartment and draws in the sophisticated crowds for weekly wine tastings. **GOYA** (357 Xinhua Lu, tel. 021/6280–1256) is a dark, cozy martini bar with couches, great drinks from an endless list, and acid jazz in the background. For glamour, go to **M ON THE BUND** (20 Guangdong Lu, tel. 021/6350–9988). The latenight lounge at **PARK 97** (Fuxing Gongyuan, 2 Gaolan Lu, tel. 021/6318–0785) is ever so chic.

Want to go American? Shanghai's **HARD ROCK CAFÉ** (1376 Nanjing Xilu, tel. 021/6279–8133) has the latest loud DJs, live pop and rock music, and crowds of Chinese yuppies. **JURASSIC PUB** (8 Maoming Nanlu, tel. 021/6253–4627 or 021/6258–3758) lives up to its Spielberg-inspired name with dinosaur skeletons wrapped around a central bar beneath a willow tree. In the Shanghai Center, the narrow, horseshoe-shape **LONG BAR** (1376 Nanjing Xilu, tel. 021/6279–8268) has a loyal expat-businessman clientele and an eclectic jukebox. The sports bar **MALONE'S AMERICAN CAFÉ** (257 Tongren Lu, tel. 021/6247–2400) has TVs broadcasting sports events, pool tables, darts, sports legend decor, and live Chinese bands covering rock 'n' roll.

If you find yourself across the river in Pudong, try the **DUBLIN EXCHANGE** (Senmao Bldg., 101 Yincheng Donglu, Pudong, tel. 021/6841–2052), with its upmarket Irish banker's club ambience, caters to the growing Wall Street that is Lujiazui. Locals love **O'MALLEY'S** (42 Taojiang Lu, tel. 021/6474–4533), which has

Guinness on tap, Irish music, and a great outdoor garden. The gigantic German beerhouse **PAULANER BRAUHAUS** (150 Fengyang Lu, tel. 021/6474–5700) and its Filipino band is a favorite among young Chinese white-collar types.

Clubs

Weekends at the casual **JUDY'S TOO** (176 Maoming Nanlu, tel. 021/6473–1417), a beautiful two-level café with a strong old-Shanghai colonial theme, can get meat-markety as the dance floor fills up with a mix of Chinese and foreigners. Shanghai's new trendiness is represented to the extreme at **MGM** (141 Shaanxi Nanlu, tel. 021/6467–3353), where the dance floor is always full of beautiful and stylish young men and women.

The vast **REAL LOVE** (10 Hengshan Lu, tel. 021/6474–6830) is becoming the late-night spot, with its postmodern decor and young nouveau-riche Shanghainese clamoring to get to the dance floor. **ROJAM DISCO** (4/F Hong Kong Plaza, 283 Huaihai Zhonglu, tel. 021/6390–7181), a three-level techno behemoth, bulges with boogiers and underground lounge lizards. The small, mellow **YING YANG (YY)** (125 Nanchang Lu, tel. 021/6431–2668 or 021/6466–4098) club, lined with black velvet and illuminated with blue light, draws an eclectic crowd of foreign yuppies and Shanghai alternative types.

Hotel Bars

At the Pudong Shangri-La's **B.A.T.S.** (33 Fucheng Lu, tel. 021/6882–8888), lively fun erupts around a central bar, with a great house band performing rhythm and blues, funk, or rock. When the weather's nice, you can get a cool drink at the **GARDEN HOTEL** terrace (58 Maoming Nanlu, tel. 021/6415–1111). The **PEACE HOTEL** rooftop (20 Nanjing Xilu, tel. 021/6321–6888) is especially romantic. The Hilton's **PENTHOUSE BAR** (250 Huashan Lu, tel. 021/6248–0000) offers a quiet, elegant drink overlooking a great view of the city. The Grand Hyatt's luxurious and jazzy **PIANO BAR** (Jinmao Dasha, 177 Lujiazui Lu, Pudong, tel. 021/5830–3338) has superb views. Cigar smoke and jazz cap the elite atmosphere at the Portman Ritz-Carlton's **RITZ-CARLTON BAR** (1376 Nanjing Xilu, tel. 021/6279–8888).

Karaoke

Karaoke TV (KTV) culture in China includes "KTV girls" who sing along with (male) guests and serve cognac and expensive snacks (at some establishments, KTV girls are also prostitutes). One of Shanghai's most popular KTV establishments is the giant **CASH BOX** (457 Wulumuqi Lu, tel. 021/6374–1111; 68 Zhejiang Nanlu, tel. 021/6374–9909; 208 Chongqing Nanlu, inside Fuxing Park, tel. 021/6358–3888). The **GOLDEN AGE** (918 Huaihai Zhonglu, tel. 021/6415–8818) is a huge, mind-boggling operation with a wealthy clientele.

THE ARTS

Acrobatics

China's best, the **SHANGHAI ACROBATIC TROUPE** performs remarkable feats and stunts at the Shanghai Center Theater (1376 Nanjing Xilu, tel. 021/6279–8663; daily 7:15 PM).

Art and Architecture

In addition to the not-to-be-missed Shanghai Museum, a number of places exhibit Chinese art. For traditional Chinese art, check out the gallery of the **GUO TAI AUCTION HOUSE** (1298 Lujiabang Lu, tel. 021/6210–1098), which holds auctions of traditional Chinese calligraphy and paintings by promising young artists on the eighth of every month at 2 PM. The **LIU HAISU ART MUSEUM** (1660 Hongqiao Lu, tel. 021/6270–1018), named after the famous Chinese traditional painter, holds regular exhibitions.

If you really want to be where it's at, get familiar with Shanghai's young contemporary avant-garde artists, who are garnering increasing world attention, at **SHANGHART** (Park 97, 2 Gaolan Lu, tel. 021/6359–3923 or 1391747857, fax 021/5403–1602), the city's first modern art gallery. It's the place to check out the work of art-world movers and shakers such as Ding Yi, Xue Song, Zhou Tiehai, Wu Yiming, and Shen Fan.

If you want to learn more about all that old architecture you're seeing on the streets or maybe take home a photography book chronicling Shanghai's history, have a cup of coffee at the ever-so-charming **OLD CHINAHAND READING ROOM** (27 Shaoxing Lu, tel. 021/6473–2526). This artistic café that looks like grandma's living room is run by Shanghainese photographer Erh Dongqiang, who has a library of history, architecture, art, literature, and coffee-table books.

Chinese Opera

Not only Beijing opera, but also China's other regional operas, such as Huju, Kunju, and Shaoxing, are performed regularly at the **YIFU THEATRE** (701 Fuzhou Lu, tel. 021/6351–4668). Call the box office for schedule and ticket information. On Sundays at 1:30 PM, students from the **SHANGHAI SCHOOL OF MUSIC AND OPERA** perform a selection of acts from different operas at the Yifu Theatre. Ticket prices range from Y5 to Y20. The **KUNJU OPERA TROUPE** (9 Shaoxing Lu, tel. 021/6437–1012) holds matinee performances every Saturday at 1:30 PM.

Dance and Music

The modern **SHANGHAI CENTER THEATER** (1376 Nanjing Xilu, tel. 021/6279–8663) is one of the chief venues in town for quality performances. The spectacular **GRAND THEATRE** (300 Renmin Dadao, tel. 021/6372–8701, 6372–8702, or 6372–3833) stages the greatest number of domestic and international classical music and ballet performances.

Not a Night Owl?

You can learn a lot about a place if you take its pulse after dark. So even if you're the original early-to-bed type, there's every reason to vary your routine when you're away from home.

EXPERIENCE THE FAMILIAR IN A NEW PLACE Whether your thing is going to the movies or going to concerts, it's always different away from home. In clubs, new faces and new sounds add up to a different scene. Or you may catch movies you'd never see at home.

TRY SOMETHING NEW Do something you've never done before. It's another way to dip into the local scene. A simple suggestion: Go out later than usual—go dancing late and finish up with breakfast at dawn.

DO SOMETHING OFFBEAT Look into lectures and readings as well as author appearances in book stores. You may even meet your favorite novelist.

EXPLORE A DAYTIME NEIGHBORHOOD AT NIGHT Take a nighttime walk through an explorable area you've already seen by day. You'll get a whole different view of it.

ASK AROUND If you strike up a conversation with like-minded people during the course of your day, ask them about their favorite spots. Your hotel concierge is another resource.

DON'T WING IT As soon as you've nailed down your travel dates, look into local publications or surf the Net to see what's on the calendar while you're in town. Look for hot regional acts, dance and theater, big-name performing artists, expositions, and sporting events. Then call or click to order tickets.

CHECK OUT THE NEIGHBORHOOD Whenever you don't know the neighborhood you'll be visiting, review safety issues with people in your hotel. What's the transportation situation? Can you walk there, or do you need a cab? Is there anything else you need to know?

CASH OR CREDIT? Know before you go. It's always fun to be surprised—but not when you can't cover your check.

Asian and Western acts sporadically appear at the **SHANGHAI GYMNASIUM** (1111 Caoxi Beilu, tel. 021/6473–0940). The **MAJESTIC THEATRE** (66 Jiangning Lu, tel. 021/6217–4409) hosts both Asian and Western performances.

The **JINGAN HOTEL** (370 Huashan Lu, San Diego Hall, tel. 021/6248–1888 Ext. 687) has regular chamber music performances. The **SHANGHAI CONCERT HALL** (523 Yanan Donglu, tel. 021/6386–9153) regularly presents classical ensembles and orchestras, mostly domestic. The **Shanghai Symphony Orchestra** performs here Saturday evening at 7:15.

Theater

Modern theater in China is primarily dominated by state-run companies. The **SHANGHAI PEOPLE'S ART THEATRE** (201 Anfu Lu, tel. 021/6431–3523) presents regular performances of Chinese plays, as well as foreign plays in Chinese translation. The **SHANGHAI THEATRE ACADEMY** (630 Huashan Lu, tel. 021/6248–2920 Ext. 3040) has three stages that periodically present student and professional works.

In This Chapter

Updated by Paul Davidson

where to stay

SINCE THE EARLY 1990S the number of foreign hotels has exploded, pushing up the standards and quality of domestic-run hotels as well. Hotels here are now approaching Western standards, and there are some classy new establishments. Shanghai's hotels cater mostly to business travelers and can be divided into two categories: modern Western-style hotels that are elegant and nicely appointed or hotels built in the city's glory days that became state-run after 1949. The latter may lack great service, modern fixings, and convenient facilities, but they make up for it in charm, tradition, and history. All hotels have cashier counters where you can change foreign currency into yuan. Again, tipping is not mandatory.

CATEGORY	COST*	
$$$$	over Y1500	over US$180
$$$	Y1275–Y1500	US$150–$180
$$	Y650–Y1275	US$80–$150
$	under Y650	under US$80

Prices are for a standard double room with bath at peak season unless otherwise stated; 15% service charge is not included.

NANJING LU AND THE BUND

$$$$ **SHANGHAI JC MANDARIN.** The 30-story blue glass towers of this hotel rise up east of the Shanghai Exhibition Center. In the lobby is a five-story-high hand-painted mural depicting the voyage of the Ming dynasty admiral Zheng Ho, as well as a coffee shop that serves great Southeast Asian food. Rooms are bright with earthy tones and natural wood. The Mandarin Club Lounge comprises the executive floors at the top of the hotel. The Cantonese restaurant has fine dim sum at affordable prices. 1225 Nanjing Xilu, 200040, tel. 021/6279–1888, fax 021/6279–1822, www.jcmandarin.com. 564 rooms, 36 suites. 4 restaurants, bar, deli, pool, sauna, tennis court, gym, squash, dance club, billiards, shops, business services, meeting room. AE, DC, MC, V.

$$$ HOTEL SOFITEL HYLAND. The only hotel directly on the Nanjing Lu pedestrian walkway, the Hyland is ideal for exploring the city center, shopping, and taking trips to the Bund. The 34-story Japanese-owned and French-managed hotel has eight floors of rooms designed specifically for business travelers. The top-floor Sky Lounge offers good views of downtown and a pleasant Sunday brunch. 505 Nanjing Donglu, 200001, tel. 021/6351–5888, fax 021/6351–4088, www.cbw.com/hotel/sofitel. 389 rooms and suites. 4 restaurants, bar, deli, hair salon, gym, shops, business services, meeting room. AE, DC, MC, V.

$$$ PORTMAN RITZ-CARLTON. ★ Its location in the Shanghai Center, along with its outstanding facilities and furnishings, draws people to this 50-story luxury hotel. Rooms have a modern East-meets-West decor, with wooden Ming-influenced furniture. It's elegant if a bit impersonal. The health club is comprehensive. The hotel has four good food outlets, plus the Portman Deli in the supermarket. 1376 Nanjing Xilu, 200040, tel. 021/6279–8888, fax 021/6279–8887, www.ritzcarlton.com. 492 rooms, 72 suites. 4 restaurants, 2 bars, indoor and outdoor pool, hair salon, sauna, tennis court, gym, racquetball, squash, dance club, shops, business services, meeting room. AE, DC, MC, V.

$$–$$$ PEACE HOTEL. ★ This romantic hotel is among Shanghai's most treasured historic buildings. Its high ceilings, ornate woodwork, and art deco fixtures are intact, and the ballroom evokes old Shanghai cabarets and gala parties, though the rooms are no longer glamorous and even tend to be a bit stuffy. Built in 1906 by the British, the south building, formerly the Palace Hotel, is the oldest structure on the Bund. The more popular north building, formerly the Cathay Hotel, built in 1929, was known as the private playground of its owner, Victor Sassoon. The eighth-floor Dragon and Phoenix Room is a good choice for dinner, while the rooftop bar is one of the most romantic spots in Shanghai. *20 Nanjing Donglu, 200002, tel. 021/6321–6888, fax 021/6329–0300, www. shanghaipeacehotel.com. 411 rooms and 9 suites. 3 restaurants, 2 bars, hair salon, gym, shops, billiards, business services, meeting room. AE, DC, MC, V.*

$$ PARK HOTEL. This historic 1934 art deco structure overlooking People's Park was once among Shanghai's more luxurious and fashionable hotels. It was completely renovated to recapture its pre-1949 glory, and it still has a musty charm, but the service and facilities are definitely second-rate. *170 Nanjing Xilu, 200003, tel. 021/6327–5225, fax 021/6327–6958. 215 rooms. 3 restaurants, hair salon, dance club, shop, business services. AE, DC, MC, V.*

OLD FRENCH CONCESSION

$$$$ GARDEN HOTEL. Managed by the Japanese Okura Group, this
★ 33-story hotel is beautifully appointed, presenting luxury with a cool Japanese aesthetic. The first three floors, which were once old Shanghai's French Club, have been renovated with many of the former art deco fixtures and frescoes still intact. The third-floor terrace, overlooking the huge garden, is a great place for a romantic drink. The hotel is also known for its excellent—and high-priced—Japanese food. The rooms are spacious and tastefully decorated. *58 Maoming Lu, 200020, tel. 021/6415–1111, fax 021/ 6415–8866, www.gardenhotelshanghai.com. 478 rooms, 22 suites. 4 restaurants, 3 bars, pool, hair salon, sauna, tennis, gym, shops, business services, meeting room. AE, DC, MC, V.*

$$$$ REGAL INTERNATIONAL EAST ASIA HOTEL. This hotel is connected to the exclusive Shanghai International Tennis Center and hotel guests can play on one of ten tennis courts. The stout hotel has a large, rather austere lobby. The rooms are large and modern, though a little bland. The main attraction is the hotel's extravagant Club House—one of the best gyms in town. *516 Hengshan Lu, 200040, tel. 021/6415–5588, fax 021/6445–8899, www.regal-*

eastasia.com. 300 rooms. 3 restaurants, bakery, hair salon, sauna, pool, tennis court, squash, gym, bowling, billiards, shops, business services, meeting room. AE, DC, MC, V.

$$$–$$$$ **HOLIDAY INN CROWNE PLAZA.** This hotel on the western side of the French Concession is known for its service. The staff here is among the friendliest in town and makes guests, mostly business travelers, feel right at home. Although a bit outside the city center, the hotel is still close to the Huaihai Lu shopping district and the Hongqiao area. The comfortable guest rooms and suites are bright and homey. 400 Panyu Lu, 200052, tel. 021/6280–8888, fax 021/6280–2788, www.sixcontinentshotels.com/holiday-inn. 467 rooms, 29 suites. 4 restaurants, bar, deli, pool, hair salon, sauna, tennis court, gym, business services, meeting room. AE, DC, MC, V.

$$$ **HUATING HOTEL AND TOWERS.** Just southwest of the old French Concession, in the Xujiahui area, the first Western hotel to open in Shanghai is a former Sheraton property. Some of the interior is a bit kitschy, while the exterior looks like an S-shape tiered wedding cake. Rooms and suites are modern and comfortable. The Towers make up the hotel's executive floors. 1200 Caoxi Beilu, 200030, tel. 021/6439–1000, fax 021/6255–0830, www.huating.com/hotel. 1,008 rooms, 56 suites. 4 restaurants, bar, pool, tennis court, bowling, gym, squash, shops, billiards, dance club, business services, meeting room. AE, DC, MC, V.

$$–$$$ **HILTON SHANGHAI.** The 43-story triangular building has some
★ of the best dining in town and top-rate accommodations. Rooms are modern and luxurious, with marble bathrooms. There are four executive floors, as well as two floors decorated in a Japanese style. The hotel coffee shop has a lovely sunlit atrium. The view from the top-floor Penthouse Bar and Sichuan Court is spectacular, a great place for watching fireworks on Chinese New Year. 250 Huashan Lu, 200040, tel. 021/6248–0000, fax 021/6248–3848, www.hilton.com. 754 rooms and 21 suites. 7 restaurants, 2 bars, deli, pool, hair salon, sauna, tennis court, gym, squash, billiards, shops, business services, meeting room. AE, DC, MC, V.

\$\$–\$\$\$ JINJIANG HOTEL. The former Cathay Mansions, Grosvenor Gardens, and Grosvenor House, now known collectively as the Jinjiang Hotel, are among the few art deco buildings left standing in the city. The Cathay was built as an apartment building in 1928 and the glamorous Grosvenor House three years later. All rooms in the latter have been left in their original design, with the beautiful art deco ornamentation intact. Standard rooms in the North Building—comfortable, traditionally furnished, and homey but not luxurious—also have an old-Shanghai feeling. The once-verdant central lawn has been replaced by a huge health center. *59 Maoming Lu, 200020, tel. 021/6258–2582, fax 021/6472–5588, www.jinjianghotelshanghai.com. 487 rooms, 28 suites. 5 restaurants, bar, hair salon, health club, sauna, shops, dance club, business services, meeting room. AE, MC, V.*

\$–\$\$ RUIJIN GUESTHOUSE. The Morriss Estate, now Ruijin Guesthouse, was built by a Western newspaper magnate. Today the estate's houses still stand amid huge green lawns and trees. Five old villas have rooms renovated in traditional Chinese style. You can have a cup of tea on the lawn on the south side of the main mansion or dine at one of the Western restaurants on the grounds. Stroll around the estate to view the ornate details, including a stained-glass window in the rear house. *118 Ruijin Er Lu, 200020, tel. 021/6472–5222, fax 021/6473–2277, www.shedi.net.cn/OUTEDI/Ruijin. 71 rooms. 5 restaurants, 3 bars, hair salon, business services. AE, DC, MC, V.*

\$ LONGHUA HOTEL. This hotel, within the walls of the Longhua Temple, caters to followers of Buddhism, but is open to everyone. Directed by the master abbot Ming Yang, the hotel is simply decorated in a Chinese style tinged with modern Western influences and post-1949 Communist starkness. The hotel's labyrinthine halls are fashioned according to traditional Chinese architecture and beliefs. Along with Chinese and Western cuisine, the hotel also serves Buddhist vegetarian dishes. *2787 Longhua Lu, 200232, tel. 021/6457–0570, fax 021/6457–7621. 140 rooms and suites. 3 restaurants, hair salon, billiards. AE, DC, MC, V.*

shanghai lodging

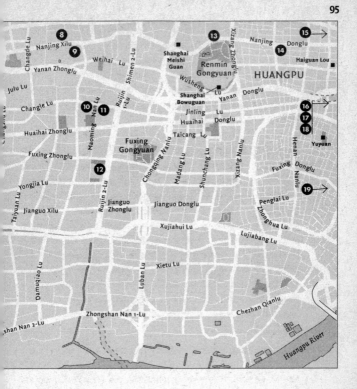

Changde Lu

Nanjing Xilu ⑧

⑨

Weihai Lu

Yanan Zhonglu

Shanghai Meishi Guan

Renmin Gongyuan ⑬

Nanjing Donglu ⑮

⑭

Haiguan Lou

HUANGPU

Julu Lu

Changle Lu

Shimen 2-Lu

Ruijin 1-Lu

Wusheng Lu

Shanghai Bowuguan

Yanan Donglu

Huaihai Zhonglu

⑩ ⑪

Maoming Nan Lu

Jinling Lu

Huaihai Donglu

⑯

⑰

Fuxing Zhonglu

Fuxing Gongyuan

Taicang Lu

⑱

Yuyuan

Yongjia Lu

⑫

Chongqing Nanlu

Madang Lu

Shunchang Lu

Xizang Nanlu

Henan Nanlu

Fuxing Donglu

⑲

Taiyuan Lu

Jianguo Xilu

Ruijin 2-Lu

Jianguo Zhonglu

Jianguo Donglu

Penglai Lu

Zhonghua Lu

Xujiahui Lu

Lujiabang Lu

Damuqiao Lu

Luban Lu

Xietu Lu

Chezhan Qianlu

shan Nan 2-Lu

Zhongshan Nan 1-Lu

Huangpu River

$ XINGGUO GUEST HOUSE. This collection of old Shanghai villas, furnished in both traditional and western styles, sits around a huge green lawn. The service and food are not as good as at Western hotels, but the quaint atmosphere definitely has more charm. Both restaurants serve Chinese cuisine. *72 Xingguo, 200052, tel. 021/6212–9998, fax 021/6251–2145. 2 restaurants, business services. AE, DC, MC, V.*

HONGQIAO DEVELOPMENT ZONE

$$$ WESTIN TAI PING YANG. This luxurious Japanese-managed high-rise hotel is extremely formal, and everything is done with a flourish. The hotel is within easy reach of the Shanghai International Exhibition Center and Shanghai Mart; Honqiao Airport is only a short ride away. Rooms are fresh and equipped with high-tech electronic amenities such as fax and data ports. Good Italian food can be found at Giovanni's, and the deli on the second floor offers a great selection of pastas, cold cuts, and breads. *5 Zunyi Nanlu, 200335, tel. 021/6275–8888, fax 021/6275–5420, www.westin-shanghai.com. 541 rooms, 39 suites. 5 restaurants, deli, pool, hair salon, sauna, tennis court, gym, shops, billiards, business services, meeting room. AE, DC, MC, V.*

$$–$$$ YANGTZE NEW WORLD HOTEL. This hotel is adjacent to the International Trade and Exhibition Center and Shanghai Mart. It has an excellent Chinese restaurant and a New York–inspired bar, Graffiti's, with live music on the weekends. The spacious rooms all have data ports and modern amenities. *2099 Yanan Xilu, 200335, tel. 021/6275–0000, fax 021/6275–0750, www.newworldhotels.com/SHANW. 553 rooms and suites. 5 restaurants, deli, pool, hair salon, sauna, gym, shops, dance club, business services, meeting room. AE, DC, MC, V.*

$$–$$$ CYPRESS HOTEL. Once part of tycoon Victor Sassoon's estate, the beautiful, expansive grounds here are filled with trees, streams, bridges, and lawns. The recently renovated rooms are simple but comfortable, with modern and electronic amenities. *2419 Hongqiao Lu, 200335, tel. 021/6268–8868, fax 021/6242–8178. 149 rooms. 5* restaurants, 2 bars, pool, sauna, tennis court, bowling, gym, squash, billiards, business services, meeting room. AE, DC, MC, V.

PUDONG NEW AREA

$$$$ **GRAND HYATT.** Occupying floors 53 through 88 of the spectacular
★ Jinmao Tower, the Grand Hyatt is the world's highest hotel. A combination of traditional and postmodern design, the Hyatt's interior is defined by art deco lines juxtaposed with space-age grillwork and sleek furnishings and textures. The 30-story central atrium is a marvel in itself—a seemingly endless cylinder with an outer-space aura. Views from the rooms are spectacular; corner rooms have two walls of pure glass for endless panoramas of the city below, and from a marble bathtub you can look at the Oriental Pearl Tower. Amenities are space age as well: CAT 5 optical lines for laptop use, Internet connections on the TV through a cordless keyboard, and three high-pressure water heads in the shower. *Jinmao Dasha, 2 Shiji Dadao, Pudong 200121, tel. 021/5049–1234, fax 021/5049–1111, www.shanghai.hyatt.com. 511 rooms, 44 suites. 5 restaurants, 3 bars, pool, hair salon, sauna, gym, shops, billiards, business services, meeting room. AE, DC, MC, V.*

$$$$ **PUDONG SHANGRI-LA.** One of the most finely appointed
★ properties in Shanghai, it overlooks the Huangpu River opposite the Bund, on the edge of Lujiazui. Next to the Pudong ferry terminal, the hotel also offers breathtaking, right-above-water-level views of the Bund, especially from its outdoor patio. The rooms have cream walls, marble bathrooms, and elm-colored furniture. The hotel has Chinese and Japanese restaurants, and a great bar-disco with rocking bands. *33 Fucheng Lu, Pudong 200120, tel. 021/6882–8888, fax 021/6882–6688, www.shangri-la.com/eng. 587 rooms and 25 suites. 5 restaurants, bar, pool, hair salon, sauna, tennis, gym, squash, shops, billiards, nightclub, business services, meeting room. AE, DC, MC, V.*

$$$ **HOLIDAY INN PUDONG.** The second Holiday Inn in Shanghai, in the commercial district of Pudong, is well situated for travelers with business in the area. The rooms are tidy and bright and all have data ports. The hotel's Irish pub Flanagan's serves Guinness

Hotel How-Tos

Where you stay does make a difference. Do you prefer a modern high-rise or an intimate B&B? A center-city location or the quiet suburbs? What facilities do you want? Sort through your priorities, then price it all out.

HOW TO GET A DEAL After you've chosen a likely candidate or two, phone them directly and price a room for your travel dates. Then call the hotel's toll-free number and ask the same questions. Also try consolidators and hotel-room discounters. You won't hear the same rates twice. On the spot, make a reservation as soon as you are quoted a price you want to pay.

PROMISES, PROMISES If you have special requests, make them when you reserve. Get written confirmation of any promises.

SETTLE IN Upon arriving, make sure everything works—lights and lamps, TV and radio, sink, tub, shower, and anything else that matters. Report any problems immediately. And don't wait until you need extra pillows or blankets or an ironing board to call housekeeping. Also check out the fire emergency instructions. Know where to find the fire exits, and make sure your companions do, too.

IF YOU NEED TO COMPLAIN Be polite but firm. Explain the problem to the person in charge. Suggest a course of action. If you aren't satisfied, repeat your requests to the manager. Document everything: Take pictures and keep a written record of who you've spoken with, when, and what was said. Contact your travel agent, if he made the reservations.

KNOW THE SCORE When you go out, take your hotel's business cards (one for everyone in your party). If you have extras, you can give them out to new acquaintances who want to call you.

TIP UP FRONT For special services, a tip or partial tip in advance can work wonders.

USE ALL THE HOTEL RESOURCES A concierge can make difficult things easy. But a desk clerk, bellhop, or other hotel employee who's friendly, smart, and ambitious can often steer you straight as well. A gratuity is in order if the advice is helpful.

and Kilkenny on tap. *899 Dongfang Lu, Pudong 200120, tel. 021/5830–6666, fax 021/5830–5555, www.sixcontinentshotels.com/holiday-inn. 320 rooms, 40 suites. 5 restaurants, bar, pool, health club, hair salon, sauna, business services, meeting room. AE, DC, MC, V.*

$$$ SHANGHAI NEW ASIA TOMSON HOTEL. The first luxury hotel in Pudong is in the heart of the Lujiazui financial district. The *pièce de résistance* of the 24-story Shanghai-Taiwan joint venture is a nearly 200-ft-high Italian Renaissance–inspired atrium with an interior garden that brings in natural light to 18 floors of elegant and spacious guest rooms. There are three executive floors, and restaurants for every taste—Italian, Swiss, Cantonese, Shanghainese, Chaozhou, and Continental. Guests have access to the 18-hole course at the Tomson Golf Club in Pudong. *777 Zhangyang Lu, Pudong 200120, tel. 021/5831–8888, fax 021/5831–7777, www.shedi.net.cn/OUTEDI/NewAsia. 344 rooms, 78 suites. 7 restaurants, bar, indoor pool, hair salon, sauna, gym, shops, billiards, nightclub, business services, meeting room. AE, DC, MC, V.*

Updated by Paul Davidson

side trip to suzhou

IF THE RENOWNED GARDENS of Suzhou form a thriving monument to the city's past, the passages leading up to them speak of a time of transition. Entire blocks of old-style houses still line some of the city's canals. Decorated gates and doorways from centuries ago catch the eye, but they now lead into shops selling silk and cashmere in Chinese and Western styles; the ramshackle houses from past eras border on tall office buildings and shiny new hotels; and the sloping, tiled roofs often sit atop structures built in the last few years. This mixture of old styles with new makes Suzhou's central districts a pleasure to explore.

Suzhou's many canals once formed the basis of its economy. Now falling into disuse, the waterways still line many a lamplighted street. These canals, however, are really only the younger cousins of the Da Yunhe (Grand Canal), which passes through the outskirts of town. Just 5 km (3 mi) south of the city is the Baodai Qiao (Precious Belt Bridge), one of the most famous and grandiose bridges on the canal. The canal used to be a main transportation route for eastern China but has been gradually replaced with newer, faster modes. The section south of Suzhou is still navigable and navigated; you can take an overnight boat (CITS; Shiquan Lu 115, tel. 0512/522–2401) to explore the canal more thoroughly.

Suzhou's main claim to fame is its fabulous array of gardens, which set a style and standard for gardens throughout the country. They were originally created by retired officials or unaffiliated literati as places in which to read and write poetry and philosophy, to stroll and drink with their friends, and to

suzhou

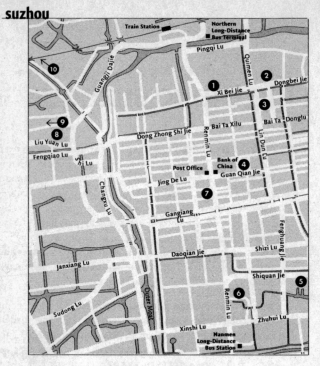

meditate and spend quiet hours. The attraction of these gardens goes beyond the mazes of bizarre rock formations or the thoughtfully arranged vegetation; rather, each garden is meant to be enjoyed for its overall atmosphere, as well as for its unique style and layout. Sit in a teahouse near the pond and feel the peaceful breeze as you watch it ruffle the water, carrying fragrances with it.

Pathways lead to an artfully planted tree winding its way up the garden wall, a glimpse of lake from a small man-made cave, a pavilion displaying Qing dynasty tree-root furniture. Every plant, rock, bit of water, piece of furniture, wall, and even fish has been carefully created or chosen for its individual shape, color, shadow, and other characteristics and for the way each blends with the whole at different times of the day and year. Although spring is considered prime viewing time, each season works its own magic.

EXPLORING

A Good Walk

Starting where Renmin Lu meets Xibei Jie in the northern section of town, check out the tall **BEISI TA** ① (North Temple Pagoda), with views of the city. Walk east along the restored street with its traditional-style fronts and shops until you come to the **ZHUO ZHENG YUAN** ② (Humble Administrator's Garden), Suzhou's largest garden. Then turn south along Yuan Lin Lu, checking out the silk shops that line the street. **SHIZI LIN** ③ (Lion's Grove Garden), filled with caves, will be on your right about halfway down the short street. At the end of the street turn right and then left onto Lindun Lu; follow that south to Guanqian Lu and turn right to reach the **XUANMIAO GUAN** ④ (Temple of Mystery), an ancient temple in a market square. Make your way down to Fenghuang Jie and for the small, exquisite **WANGSHI YUAN** ⑤ (Master of the Nets head south to Shiquan Jie, turning left Garden). From here go left on Shiquan Jie to Renmin Lu, turn left again and follow it to **CANGLANG TING** ⑥ (Blue Wave Pavilion), a large garden off the street to the left. Back up Renmin Lu, just north of Ganjiang Lu, stop to visit a newer garden, **YI YUAN** ⑦ (Joyous Garden). Take a bus or taxi north and west across the city moat and a branch of the Grand Canal to the large, well-designed **LIU YUAN** ⑧ (Lingering Garden). Just to the west, at the end of Liuyuan Lu, is the Buddhist **XI YUAN SI** ⑨ (West Garden Temple). From Xi Yuan Si, take another taxi or the No. 5 bus to **HUQIU** ⑩ (Tiger Hill), a large park north of the city with a leaning pagoda.

The most leisurely way to do this walk is to spread it out over two days.

Sights to See

❶ **BEISI TA** (North Temple Pagoda). A pagoda has stood on these grounds since the Three Kingdoms Period, though the existing pagoda dates from 1153. You can climb as high as the eighth floor of the nine-story structure to get what might be the best view (still) of Suzhou. There are large windows and balconies on each floor. The grounds form a garden of their own (though not a very good one), and there's an art gallery behind the pagoda. *Xibei Jie and Renmin Lu. Y10; Y5 to climb the pagoda. Daily 7:45–6.*

❻ **CANGLANG TING** (Blue Wave Pavilion). In one of Suzhou's largest and oldest gardens you can thread your way through a maze of oddly shaped doorways, around an artificial pond, and into a large, man-made cave with a small stone picnic table. The garden was originally built in the 10th century and, although lovely in its own way, is not as delicately wrought as some of the smaller gardens. *Off Renmin Lu between Shiquan Jie and Xinshi Lu. Y8. Daily 8–5.*

❿ **HUQIU** (Tiger Hill). Five kilometers (three miles) northwest of the city center stands this park, home of the tomb of Helu, the supposed founder of the city. According to legend, a white tiger appeared here three days after he was interned, hence the name.

Also here is **Xia Ta** (Leaning Pagoda), Suzhou's version of the Leaning Tower of Pisa, tilting at a 15° angle. *Huqiu Lu, north of city.* Y25. *Daily 7:30–5:30.*

8 **LIU YUAN** (Lingering Garden). In the western part of the city is another of Suzhou's larger gardens, originally installed during the Ming dynasty. Paths wind around a small pond area and through some impressive rock formations. Several pavilions are set around the park, inside of which are calligraphy expositions. Beyond the park's outer wall is a nursery with scores of carefully tended bonsai trees. *Liuyuan Lu. Y16. Daily 8–5.*

3 **SHIZI LIN** (Lion's Grove Garden). Here a labyrinth of man-made caves surrounds a small scenic lake. Its wall is divided and its pavilions are sited to make the garden seem more spacious than it really is. The illusions of space are expertly created here, and the bridges on the lake provide many a couple with a romantic photo op. You can get a wide view of the garden walking the paths around the lake, while the cave maze brings your attention to minute landscaping details. A tearoom on the second floor of the main pavilion overlooks the lake. At the garden's exit is a small marketplace with antique replicas and silks of all sorts. *23 Yuan Lin Lu, Y10. Daily 7:30–5.*

★ **5** **WANGSHI YUAN** (Master of the Nets Garden). Despite its comparatively small size, Wangshi Yuan, with its subdued beauty, is the most interesting garden in a city famous for its gardens. All of the elements of the Suzhou style are here—artificial rock hills, an abundance of flora, pavilions overlooking a central pond—in seemingly perfect balance, as if this were the culmination of the art of garden design. The park was originally constructed in the 12th century, and reworked in the 18th. The former living quarters now house exhibits of Qing dynasty tree-root furniture and some fine pieces of traditional ink painting and calligraphy. One placard announces that the **Dianchun Yi** (Spring Cottage) was reproduced for an exhibition in the Metropolitan Museum of Art in New York. *Shiquan Jie, tel. 0512/520–3514. Day, Y10; evening, Y60. Daily 8–5 and 7:30–10.*

❾ XI YUAN SI (West Garden Temple). This Buddhist temple was originally constructed in the Yuan dynasty, although the current building dates from the 19th century (Qing dynasty). Behind the main temple is the Xihua garden, a large open area with several ponds. Of particular interest is the **Wubai Luohan Tang** (Hall of 500 Arhats), which houses 500 gold-painted statues of arhats, each with its own peculiar expression. *8 Xiyuan Lu (down the street from Liu Yuan). Y6. Daily 7–5.*

❹ XUANMIAO GUAN (Temple of Mystery). One of the most well-preserved old-style temples, the Temple of Mystery backs a large market square, which used to be temple grounds. Founded in the 3rd century, the Taoist temple has undergone fewer restorations than most its age, still retaining parts from the 12th century. The main building, Sanqing Dian, is one of the largest wooden structures in China. Fortunately, it suffered very little damage in the Cultural Revolution. *Guanqian Jie. Y5; additional fees for different temples. Daily 7:30–5.*

❼ YI YUAN (Joyous Garden). A more recent example of Suzhou style, this one also has a pleasant blending of pavilion and rockery, courtyard and pond. *343 Renmin Lu. Y4. Daily 7:30–5.*

❷ ZHUO ZHENG YUAN (Humble Administrator's Garden). Suzhou's largest, this 10-acre garden is renowned for its its so-called high and low architecture and expansive pond area. It was built by Wang Xianjun, an unemployed official in the Ming dynasty, who drew its name from a line in a Tang dynasty rhapsody. The line of poetry, reading "humble people govern," seems like a clever bit of sarcasm when considered in conjunction with the grand scale of this private garden—perhaps explaining Wang's unsuitability for public life. The garden is separated into three parts—east, central, and west—each with its own pavilions and pond. Near the garden's entrance is a large display of bonsai trees. *178 Dong Bei Jie. Y20. Daily 7:30–5:30.*

DINING AND LODGING

$–$$$ DEYUELOU. This restaurant which has served Suzhou-style food for more than 400 years has a wide array of fish dishes, local-style dim sum, and a particularly tasty *Deyue Tongji* (braised chicken). It also specializes in an attractive type of food presentation, the ancient art of "garden foods"—an assortment of dim sum specialties arranged to resemble various sorts of gardens, with foods portraying flowers, trees, and rocks. *27 Taijian Nong, tel. 0512/ 523–8940. AE, MC, V.*

$–$$ HUANGTIANYUAN. Here the specialty is the local favorite of *mifen* (rice gluten), made by pounding rice to a fine paste. In business since 1821, it has different seasonal menus, serving the foods traditionally considered most appropriate for specific times of year. Other house specialties include *babao fan* (syrupy rice with various sweets, nuts, and fruit bits) and *tang tuan* (a kind of dim sum whose skin is made of the thick dough of mifen). These come in a variety of sizes and with both meaty and sweet fillings. *86 Guanqian Jie, tel. 0512/728–6933. No credit cards.*

$–$$ SONGHELOU. With almost 250 years of history, this is one of Suzhou's most famous restaurants. It serves Suzhou specialties and catches from the river that in the old days were actually eaten on riverboats during banquet cruises—hence their popular designation: "boat food." The recommended dish here is the *Songshu Guiyu*, or "squirrel-shaped Mandarin fish" (don't let the English translation turn you off). The restaurant has nine dining halls decorated with Suzhou regional arts and calligraphy. *18 Taijian Nong, tel. 0512/523–7969. V.*

$$$ NANLIN HOTEL. This hotel has a quiet setting somewhat back from the road. Master of the Nets Garden and Blue Wave Pavilion are both within walking distance. *20 Gunxiu Fang, Shiquan Jie, 215006, tel. 0512/519–4641, fax 0512/519–1028, www.nanlinhotel.com.cn. 240 rooms, 12 suites. 2 restaurants, bar, hair salon, health club, business services, meeting room. AE, MC, V.*

$$–$$$ NANYUAN HOTEL. Priced just above the more budget-oriented accommodations, the Nanyuan relies on its excellent location to draw guests. It is west of Wangshi Yuan and near the most fashionable hotels in town. *249 Shiquan Jie, 215006, tel. 0512/519–7661, fax 0512/519–8806. 104 rooms, 10 suites. 2 restaurants, bar, hair salon, health club, business services, meeting room. AE, MC, V.*

$$–$$$ SUZHOU HOTEL. The service and facilities here are excellent. It's a short walk down a popular street lined with silk and cashmere stores that leads to the Master of the Nets Garden. There is a post office conveniently located next to the lobby. *115 Shiquan Jie, 215006, tel. 0512/520–4646, fax 0512/520–4015, www.suzhou-hotel.com. 280 rooms, 21 suites. 16 restaurants, 2 bars, hair salon, health club, business services, meeting room. AE, MC, V.*

$$ BAMBOO GROVE HOTEL. A modern facility, the Bamboo Grove caters to international business travelers and tourists. It is one of the city's choice establishments in terms of facilities and quality of service, though its location is somewhat out of the way. *168 Zhuhui Lu, 215006, tel. 0512/520–5601, fax 0512/520–8778. 356 rooms, 42 suites. 4 restaurants, bar, hair salon, health club, business services, meeting room. AE, MC, V.*

$–$$ LEXIANG HOTEL. Catering mainly to Chinese guests, this budget option is more basic in its approach than the hotels on fashionable Shiquan Jie. It does have a fine location, just down the street from the Joyous Garden and a block from the beautiful Temple of Mystery. *18 Dajingxiang, tel. 0512/522–2890, fax 0512/524–4165. 38 rooms, 2 suites. 2 restaurants, bar, hair salon, health club, business services, meeting room. AE, MC, V.*

NIGHTLIFE AND THE ARTS

Wangshi Yuan (The Master of the Nets Garden) has nightly **TRADITIONAL OPERA AND MUSIC PERFORMANCES** throughout the year (Y60). The show presents a taste of various scenes from opera, as well as an opportunity to hear classical Chinese instruments. It can be a bit crowded during the peak of the tourist season. The beautiful location, however, makes the performance a uniquely enjoyable experience. Check at the entrance gate of the garden or with CITS about times and tickets.

Apart from the karaoke clubs, there really are no bars to speak of outside the few uninteresting ones in Western hotels.

SHOPPING

Districts around the gardens and temples teem with silk shops and outdoor markets. The **FRIENDSHIP STORE** (504 Renmin Lu, tel. 0512/523–6165) has a selection of local products in silk, wood, and jade. Since 1956 the **SUZHOU ANTIQUES STORE** (328 Renmin Lu, near Leqiao Bridge, tel. 0512/522–8368) has been selling antiques, calligraphy, jades, and other "cultural products." You can get jewelry and carvings at the **SUZHOU JADE CARVING FACTORY** (33 Baita Xilu, tel. 0512/727–1224). The **SUZHOU SILK MUSEUM SHOP** (661 Renmin Lu, tel. 0512/ 753–4941) is really the reason to come to the Silk Museum in the first place. For local artworks and calligraphy, visit the **WUMEN ARTSTORE** (105 Liuyuan Lu, tel. 0512/533–4808).

SUZHOU A TO Z

To research prices, get advice from other travelers, and book travel arrangements, visit www.fodors.com

Boat and Ferry Travel

The overnight ride from Suzhou to Hangzhou along the Grand Canal takes you through some great countryside scenery between two of China's prettiest cities. Tickets can be purchased through your hotel or a travel agent. The Suzhou Ferry Terminal is on the south side of the city near the old city gate.

➤ **BOAT AND FERRY INFORMATION: Suzhou Ferry Terminal** (2 Renmin Lu, tel. 0512/520–6681).

Bus Travel

Frequent bus service runs between Shanghai and Suzhou, though it's not a comfortable as the train. In Shanghai, the office for Suzhou bus tickets is at the eastern end of People's Square. The Suzhou bus station is at the southern tip of Renmin Lu.

It's best to have the name of your destination written in Chinese to avoid misunderstanding.

➤ **BUS INFORMATION: Suzhou bus station** (Southern tip of Renmin Lu, tel. 0512/520–4867).

Emergencies

Suzhou's hospital is open 24 hours.

➤ **CONTACTS: People's Hospital No. 2** (26 Daoqian Jie, Suzhou, tel. 0512/522–3691).

Tours

Major hotels will often arrange a tour guide for a group, as will CITS. Individuals may offer you day tours; just make sure the price is set and the guide's English is good enough to make it worthwhile.

Train Travel

Two comfortable air-conditioned "tourist trains" run daily between Suzhou and Shanghai. The Shanghai Railway Station is in the northern part of the city. Tickets can be purchased either through your hotel or at the stations. The trip takes 1¼ hours one way.

➤ **TRAIN INFORMATION: Shanghai Railway Station** (303 Moling Lu, tel. 021/6317–9090). **Ticket office** (777 Hengfeng Lu, tel. 021/6317–0000).

Transportation around Suzhou

Taxis are plentiful and quite inexpensive and are a better bet than the crowded and confusing bus systems. Motor tricycles are inexpensive and convenient if you have only a couple of people.

Visitor Information

➤ **TOURIST INFORMATION: CITS** (115 Shiquan Lu, Suzhou, tel. 0512/522–3783). **Suzhou International Travel Service** (Fenghuang Jie, Dinghuishi Xiangkou, Suzhou, tel. 0512/511–4339). **Suzhou Taihu International Travel Service** (105 Renmin Nanlu, Suzhou, tel. 0512/510–4522).

practical information

Air Travel

BOOKING

When you book **look for nonstop flights** and **remember that "direct" flights stop at least once.** Try to avoid connecting flights, which require a change of plane. For more booking tips and to check prices and make on-line flight reservations, log on to www.fodors.com.

CARRIERS

Many offices of international carriers are represented in the Shanghai Center and Shanghai's western hotels. Major foreign airlines that serve Shanghai are: Air France, Asiana, British Airways, Dragon Airlines, Japan Airlines, Lufthansa, Malaysian Airlines, Northwest Airlines, Qantas, SAS, Singapore Airlines, Swiss Air, Thai Airlines, United Airlines, and Virgin Airlines.

Domestic carriers that connect international destinations to Shanghai include Air China and China Eastern Airlines.

A number of regional carriers serve Shanghai, but China Eastern Airlines is the main airline connecting it with other cities in China.

➤ AIRLINES AND CONTACTS: **Air France** (Shanghai Center, 1376 Nanjing Xilu, tel. 021/6279–8600). **Air China** (600 Huashan Lu, tel. 021/6327–7888). **Asiana, British Airways, Dragon Airlines** (Shanghai Center, 1376 Nanjing Xilu, tel. 021/6279–8099). **China Eastern Airlines** (200 Yanan Xilu, tel. 021/6247–5953 domestic;

021/6247–2255 international). **Japan Airlines** (Ruijin Dasha, 205 Maoming Nanlu, tel. 021/6472–3000). **Lufthansa** (Shanghai Hilton, 250 Huashan Lu, tel. 021/6248–1100). **Malaysian Airlines** (Shanghai Center, 1376 Nanjing Xilu, tel. 021/6279–8600). **Northwest Airlines** (Shanghai Center, tel. 021/6279–8088). **Qantas** (Shanghai Center, tel. 021/6279–8660). **SAS** (Jin Jiang Hotel, 59 Maoming Nanlu, tel. 021/6472–3131). **Singapore Airlines** (Shanghai Center, tel. 021/6279–8000). **Swiss Air** (Shanghai Center, tel. 021/6279–7381). **Thai Airlines** (Shanghai Center, 1376 Nanjing Xilu, tel. 021/6279–8600). **United Airlines** (Shanghai Center, tel. 021/6279–8009). **Virgin Airlines** (12 The Bund [Zhongshan Dong Yi Lu], tel. 021/5353–4600).

CHECK-IN & BOARDING

Always ask your carrier about its check-in policy. Plan to arrive at the airport about 2 hours before your scheduled departure time for domestic flights and 2½ to 3 hours before international flights.

Assuming that not everyone with a ticket will show up, airlines routinely overbook planes. When everyone does, airlines ask for volunteers to give up their seats. In return, these volunteers usually get a certificate for a free flight and are rebooked on the next flight out. If there are not enough volunteers, the airline must choose who will be denied boarding. The first to get bumped are passengers who checked in late and those flying on discounted tickets, so **get to the gate and check in as early as possible,** especially during peak periods.

Always bring a government-issued photo I.D. to the airport; even when it's not required, a passport is best.

CUTTING COSTS

The least expensive airfares to China must usually be purchased in advance and are nonrefundable. It's smart to **call a number of airlines,** and when you are quoted a good price, **book it on the spot**—the same fare may not be available the next day. Always **check different routings** and look into using different airports.

Travel agents, especially low-fare specialists (☞ Discounts & Deals), are helpful.

Consolidators are another good source. They buy tickets for scheduled international flights at reduced rates from the airlines, then sell them at prices that beat the best fare available directly from the airlines, usually without restrictions. Sometimes you can even get your money back if you need to return the ticket. Carefully read the fine print detailing penalties for changes and cancellations, and confirm your consolidator reservation with the airline.

➤ **CONSOLIDATORS: Cheap Airlines** (tel. 800/852–2608, www.cheapairlines.com). **Cheap Tickets** (tel. 800/377–1000, www.cheaptickets.com). **Discount Airline Ticket Service** (tel. 800/576–1600). **Economy Travel** (tel. 888/222–2110, www.economytravel.com). **Travelocity** (tel. 877/811–9982, www.travelocity.com). **Unitravel** (tel. 800/325–2222). **Up & Away Travel** (tel. 212/889–2345). **World Travel Network** (tel. 800/409–6753).

ENJOYING THE FLIGHT

For more legroom, **request an emergency-aisle seat.** Don't sit in the row in front of the emergency aisle or in front of a bulkhead, where seats may not recline. If you have dietary concerns, **ask for special meals when booking.** These can be vegetarian, low-cholesterol, or kosher, for example. On long flights, try to maintain a normal routine, to help fight jet lag. At night, get some sleep. By day, **eat light meals, drink water** (not alcohol), and **move around the cabin** to stretch your legs. For additional jet-lag tips consult *Fodor's FYI: Travel Fit & Healthy* (available at bookstores everywhere).

If you're flying on local carriers while traveling within China, be prepared for less leg room and smaller seats.

FLYING TIMES

Flying time to Shanghai is between 20 and 24 hours from New York, including a stopover on the West Coast or in Tokyo; from

17 to 20 hours from Chicago; and 15 to 16 hours direct from Los Angeles or San Francisco.

RECONFIRMING

Ask your airline or tour operator about its reconfirmation policy and be sure to keep this policy in mind as you travel.

Airports & Transfers

The ultramodern Pudong International Airport opened in 1999 across the river east of the city center. Many, though not all, international flights are routed through here. Hongqiao International Airport, in western Shanghai about 15 km (9 mi) from the city center, receives most domestic flights, especially those to smaller city airports. A taxi ride between the two airports will cost you about Y250 and take at least 45 minutes. Shuttle buses between the airports cost Y22 and take much longer.

➤ AIRPORT INFORMATION: **Hongqiao International Airport** (tel. 021/6268–8918 for 24-hr airport information). **Pudong International Airport** (tel. 021/3848–4500).

AIRPORT TRANSFERS

Depending on the traffic, the trip between Hongqiao International Airport and the city center can take anywhere from 30 minutes to an hour. Plenty of taxis are available at the lines right outside both the international and domestic terminals. Don't take a ride with drivers who tout their services at the terminal entrances; their cars don't have meters, and they'll try to charge you exorbitant rates. To get into the city, most drivers use the recently opened expressway that connects to the Ring Road. Expect to reimburse the driver for the toll.

Pudong Airport Shuttle Buses link the airport with a number of hotels and major sites in the city center; the trip takes about 1 hour and 20 minutes and costs about Y15–Y20, depending on the destination.

➤ **TAXIS & SHUTTLES: Pudong Airport Shuttle Buses** (tel. 021/ 6834–6912 or 021/6834–6645).

Bike Travel

Travel by bike within the city is popular. Biking around China independently is not a good idea, as foreigners are not permitted in many cities and can be penalized by police for trespassing. Biking within and around the cities is fine, as long as you don't mind maneuvering among the crowds of pedestrians, motorists, and other bicyclists. Shanghai has wide bike lanes that are separate from regular traffic.

Bikes can be rented just about everywhere, although your hotel and CITS are usually the best places to rent/inquire. When renting, you must show ID and pay a deposit. It's also prudent to **park your bike at guarded parking spaces** to avoid theft. Bike-repair shops are common.

BIKES IN FLIGHT

Most airlines accommodate bikes as luggage, provided they are dismantled and boxed. Airlines sell bike boxes, which are often free at bike shops, for about $5 (it's at least $100 for bike bags). International travelers can sometimes substitute a bike for a piece of checked luggage at no charge; otherwise, the cost is about $100.

Boat & Ferry Travel

Boats running between Shanghai and Hong Kong (2½ days) and Shanghai and Osaka and Kobe in Japan dock at Waihongqiao Harbor. Tickets can be booked through CITS. The boat to Osaka leaves every Tuesday at noon arriving in Japan at noon on Thursday. The boat to Kobe leaves every Saturday at noon and arrives in Japan at 10AM on Monday.

Most domestic boats leave from the Shiliupu Dock for such destinations on the Yangzi (Changjiang) River as Wuhan,

Chongqing, Nanjing, Wuhu, and Jiujiang, as well as for such coastal cities as Guangzhou, Qingdao, Dalian, Ningbo, and Fuzhou. Boats for the outlying island of Putuoshan leave daily. All domestic tickets can be purchased at the foreigner ticket booth on the second floor of the Boat Ticket Booking Office, as well as at CITS. River passenger transport information can be obtained from the information line.

There's a wide range of boats, although most domestic boats are not luxurious. They do, however, offer different levels of berths, the most comfortable being first class.

➤ **BOAT & FERRY INFORMATION: Boat Ticket Booking Office** (1 Jinling Donglu, tel. 021/6328–0010). **CITS** (Guangming Bldg., 2 Jinling Lu, tel. 021/6321–7200). **Passenger information** (tel. 021/6326–1261). **Shiliupu Dock** (Zhongshan Donglu just south of the Bund). **Waihongqiao Harbor** (1 Taiping Lu).

Bus Travel to & from Shanghai

Getting to and from Shanghai by bus is usually less convenient than by train. A deluxe coach bus does run between Shanghai and Nanjing (3½ hours, Y60). Regular buses, most of which lack comfort, run from the long-distance bus station. These are acceptable for shorter distances, such as to Hangzhou and Suzhou. The ticket office for Suzhou tickets (Y50 round-trip) is at the eastern end of People's Square. Check out train fares and schedules before taking the bus.

➤ **BUS INFORMATION: Deluxe coach bus** (58 Laochongqing Nanlu, tel. 021/6358–8089). **Long-distance bus station** (Qiujiang Lu west of Henan Beilu).

Bus Travel within Shanghai

Several Shanghai buses now have air-conditioning and plenty of seats. Most, though, are very old and uncomfortable, primarily standing-room only, and extremely inconvenient. Often you'll have to change buses several times to get where you're going. During busy traffic hours they're unbelievably crowded. On most buses the fare is Y1 for any stop on the line.

One exception to the above is the double-decker bus running down Huaihai Lu through the old French Concession. It's a pleasant ride, as these vehicles imported from Hong Kong and there are many seats. From the top deck, you have a great view over the compound walls of the beautiful old Shanghai buildings that line the thoroughfare. Fares on this bus line will run you a few yuan.

Business Hours

All businesses are closed on Chinese New Year and other major holidays.

BANKS & OFFICES
Banks, offices, government departments, and police stations (known as Public Security Bureaus, or PSBs) are open Monday–Saturday. Most open between 8 AM and 9 AM, close for lunch from noon to 2, and reopen until 5 or 6. Many branches of the Bank of China, China International Travel Service (CITS), and stores catering to foreigners are open Sunday morning. Some close on Wednesday afternoon.

MUSEUMS & SIGHTS
Museums are open 9 to 4 six days a week. They're usually closed on Monday.

SHOPS
Stores throughout China are generally open daily from 9 AM to 7 PM; those in touristy areas may stay open until 9 PM. Most are open on Sunday. Restaurants are usually open until 10 or 11.

Cameras & Photography

The Chinese love cameras and will be glad to take your picture—some may even want to be in them. However, you should always **ask before taking pictures of people.** Remember that at some sites photography is not allowed, and you risk a fine and/or camera seizure if you try to sneak a photo.

The *Kodak Guide to Shooting Great Travel Pictures* (available at bookstores everywhere) is loaded with tips.

➤ **PHOTO HELP: Kodak Information Center** (tel. 800/242–2424).

CUSTOMS
Before departing, **register your foreign-made camera or laptop with U.S. Customs** (☞ Customs & Duties). If your equipment is U.S.-made, call the consulate of the country you'll be visiting to find out whether the device should be registered with local customs upon arrival.

Car Rental

Car rentals are not recommended and generally not available in China. Some local rentals are now possible Shanghai, but only for driving within the city (international tourists are forbidden from driving between most cities).

➤ **MAJOR AGENCIES: Avis** (tel. 800/331–1084; 800/879–2847 in Canada; 02/9353–9000 in Australia; 09/525–1982 in New Zealand; 0870/606–0100 in the U.K., www.avis.com). **Hertz** (tel. 800/654–3001; 800/263–0600 in Canada; 020/8897–2072 in the U.K.; 02/9669–2444 in Australia; 09/256–8690 in New Zealand, www.hertz.com).

INSURANCE
When driving a rented car you are generally responsible for any damage to or loss of the vehicle as well as for any property damage or personal injury that you may cause. Before you rent,

see what coverage your personal auto-insurance policy and credit cards provide.

REQUIREMENTS & RESTRICTIONS

In China your own driver's license is not acceptable. An International Driver's Permit is available from the American or Canadian Automobile Association, or in the United Kingdom, from the Automobile Association or the Royal Automobile Club.

SURCHARGES

Before you pick up a car in one city and leave it in another, **ask about drop-off charges or one-way service fees,** which can be substantial. Note, too, that some rental agencies charge extra if you return the car before the time specified in your contract. To avoid a hefty refueling fee, **fill the tank just before you turn in the car,** but be aware that gas stations near the rental outlet may overcharge.

Car Travel

Car travel in China, even when you're in the passenger seat, can be frightening. Cars speed to pass one another on one-lane roads, constantly blaring their horns. Taxis and pedicabs pass within inches of each other at intersections. Lanes and traffic rules seem ambiguous to those not accustomed to the Chinese style of driving. In larger cities, however, taxi driver identification numbers can be used to report bad behavior or bad driving, and thus tend to inspire more care. Many taxi drivers are also held liable for the condition of their vehicles, so they are less likely to take dangerous risks.

RULES OF THE ROAD

Driving is on the right in mainland China. Traffic lights can be sparse but are obeyed. Road signs are also sparse except in cities. Traffic in the cities can move slowly, but pay attention nonetheless. Many street signs are in pinyin as well as Chinese characters.

Children in China

Cities have parks, zoos, and frequent performances involving acrobats, jugglers, and puppets. Most large international hotels have baby-sitting services and may even offer special activities, though services may not be on a level with those in the West. In addition, travel can be rugged, familiar foods hard to find, and there are health risks and sanitation problems. It's not advisable to take children on trips outside the major cities.

Check with the CITS office for activities or tours. For general advice about traveling with children, consult *Fodor's FYI: Travel with Your Baby* (available in bookstores everywhere).

FLYING

If your children are two or older, **ask about children's airfares.** As a general rule, infants under 2 not occupying a seat fly at greatly reduced fares or even for free. When booking, **confirm carry-on allowances** if you're traveling with infants. In general, for babies charged 10% of the adult fare you are allowed one carry-on bag and a collapsible stroller; if the flight is full, the stroller may have to be checked or you may be limited to less.

Experts agree that it's a good idea to use safety seats aloft for children weighing less than 40 pounds. Airlines set their own policies: U.S. carriers usually require that the child be ticketed, even if he or she is young enough to ride free, since the seats must be strapped into regular seats. Do **check your airline's policy about using safety seats during takeoff and landing.** And since safety seats are not allowed everywhere in the plane, get your seat assignments early.

When reserving, **request children's meals or a freestanding bassinet** if you need them. But note that bulkhead seats, where you must sit to use the bassinet, may lack an overhead bin or storage space on the floor.

LODGING

Most hotels in China allow children under a certain age to stay in their parents' room at no extra charge, but others charge for them as extra adults; be sure to **find out the cutoff age for children's discounts.**

PRECAUTIONS

If you're traveling with a child, be sure to take a generous supply of Pepto Bismol tablets, antibiotics such as Cipro, rehydration salts for diarrhea, motion sickness tablets, Tylenol, and vitamins. Children, like adults, will need some time to adjust to China's food, so be sure all food is thoroughly cooked. Boiled water is fine for children to drink; soybean milk, juices, and mineral water are also available.

SIGHTS & ATTRACTIONS

Places that are especially appealing to children are indicated by a rubber-duckie icon (🐤) in the margin.

Computers on the Road

Most hotels that serve foreigners allow modem hook-up from your room; you can usually access the Internet from computers in the hotel's business center as well (be prepared for very slow dial-ups). Bring a surge protector and a 220-volt adapter. While some outlets accept American plugs, it's a good idea to **carry several types of adapters** in case the Asian one (with diagonal prongs pointing inward) doesn't fit. Chinese sockets come in several different configurations.

Consulates

➤ **AUSTRALIA: Australian Consulate** (17 Fuxing Xilu, tel. 021/6433–4604).

➤ **CANADA: Canadian Consulate** (Shanghai Center, No. 604, 1376 Nanjing Xilu, tel. 021/6279–8400).

➤ **NEW ZEALAND: New Zealand Consulate** (Qihua Dasha, 15th floor, 1375 Huaihai Zhonglu, tel. 021/6433–2230).

➤ **UNITED KINGDOM: British Consulate** (Shanghai Center, No. 301, 1376 Nanjing Xilu, tel. 021/6279–7650).

➤ **UNITED STATES: United States Consulate** (1469 Huaihai Zhonglu, tel. 021/6433–6880 or 021/6433–3936; emergencies, tel. 021/6433–6880 or 021/6433–3936).

Customs & Duties

When shopping, **keep receipts** for all purchases. Upon reentering the country, **be ready to show customs officials what you've bought.** If you feel a duty is incorrect or object to the way your clearance was handled, note the inspector's badge number and ask to see a supervisor. If the problem isn't resolved, write to the appropriate authorities, beginning with the port director at your point of entry.

IN AUSTRALIA

Australian residents who are 18 or older may bring home $A400 worth of souvenirs and gifts (including jewelry), 250 cigarettes or 250 grams of tobacco, and 1,125 ml of alcohol (including wine, beer, and spirits). Residents under 18 may bring back $A200 worth of goods. Prohibited items include meat products. Seeds, plants, and fruits need to be declared upon arrival.

➤ **INFORMATION: Australian Customs Service** (Regional Director, Box 8, Sydney, NSW 2001, Australia, tel. 02/9213–2000, fax 02/9213–4000, www.customs.gov.au).

IN CANADA

Canadian residents who have been out of Canada for at least seven days may bring home C$750 worth of goods duty-free. If you've been away fewer than seven days but more than 48 hours, the duty-free allowance drops to C$200; if your trip lasts

24–48 hours, the allowance is C$50. You may not pool allowances with family members. Goods claimed under the C$750 exemption may follow you by mail; those claimed under the lesser exemptions must accompany you. Alcohol and tobacco products may be included in the seven-day and 48-hour exemptions but not in the 24-hour exemption. If you meet the age requirements of the province or territory through which you reenter Canada, you may bring in, duty-free, 1.14 liters (40 imperial ounces) of wine or liquor or 24 12-ounce cans or bottles of beer or ale. If you are 19 or older you may bring in, duty-free, 200 cigarettes and 50 cigars. Check ahead of time with the Canada Customs Revenue Agency or the Department of Agriculture for policies regarding meat products, seeds, plants, and fruits.

You may send an unlimited number of gifts worth up to C$60 each duty-free to Canada. Label the package UNSOLICITED GIFT— VALUE UNDER $60. Alcohol and tobacco are excluded.

➤ **INFORMATION: Canada Customs Revenue Agency** (2265 St. Laurent Blvd. S, Ottawa, Ontario K1G 4K3, Canada, tel. 204/983–3500 or 506/636–5064; 800/461–9999 in Canada, www.ccra-adrc.gc.ca).

IN CHINA

You will receive a short customs form either in the airplane or in the terminal on landing. Foreign currency for personal use has no restrictions. You are not allowed to bring in live animals, fresh produce, or printed matter deemed seditious or pornographic. The former is very broadly defined, of course, and would include anything that criticizes the Chinese government. They do not usually inspect your personal baggage for improper reading matter, but it could happen. It's best, for example, not to bring a book by a Chinese dissident with you. Customs inspection is usually fast and painless, unless of course you're suspected of bringing in the above-mentioned items.

On leaving, you are not allowed to take out of China antiques more than 150 years old and deemed valuable to the country.

IN NEW ZEALAND

Homeward-bound residents 17 or older may bring back $700 worth of souvenirs and gifts. Your duty-free allowance also includes 4.5 liters of wine or beer; one 1,125-ml bottle of spirits; and either 200 cigarettes, 250 grams of tobacco, 50 cigars, or a combination of the three up to 250 grams. Prohibited items include meat products, seeds, plants, and fruits.

➤ **INFORMATION: New Zealand Customs** (Custom House, 50 Anzac Ave., Box 29, Auckland, New Zealand, tel. 09/300–5399, fax 09/359–6730), www.customs.govt.nz.

IN THE U.K.

From countries outside the European Union, including China, you may bring home, duty-free, 200 cigarettes or 50 cigars; 1 liter of spirits or 2 liters of fortified or sparkling wine or liqueurs; 2 liters of still table wine; 60 ml of perfume; 250 ml of toilet water; plus £145 worth of other goods, including gifts and souvenirs. If returning from outside the EU, prohibited items include meat products, seeds, plants, and fruits.

➤ **INFORMATION: HM Customs and Excise** (Dorset House, Stamford St., Bromley, Kent BR1 1XX, U.K., tel. 020/7202–4227, www.hmce.gov.uk).

IN THE U.S.

U.S. residents who have been out of the country for at least 48 hours (and who have not used the $400 allowance or any part of it in the past 30 days) may bring home $400 worth of foreign goods duty-free.

U.S. residents 21 and older may bring back 1 liter of alcohol duty-free. In addition, regardless of your age, you are allowed 200 cigarettes and 100 non-Cuban cigars. Antiques, which the U.S.

Customs Service defines as objects more than 100 years old, enter duty-free, as do original works of art done entirely by hand, including paintings, drawings, and sculptures.

You may also mail or ship packages home duty-free: up to $200 worth of goods for personal use, with a limit of one parcel per addressee per day (except alcohol or tobacco products or perfume worth more than $5); label the package PERSONAL USE and attach a list of its contents and their retail value. Do not label the package UNSOLICITED GIFT or your duty-free exemption will drop to $100. Mailed items do not affect your duty-free allowance on your return.

➤ **INFORMATION: U.S. Customs Service** (1300 Pennsylvania Ave. NW, Room 6.3D, Washington, DC 20229, www.customs.gov; inquiries tel. 202/354–1000; complaints c/o 1300 Pennsylvania Ave. NW, Room 5.4D, Washington, DC 20229; registration of equipment c/o Office of Passenger Programs, tel. 202/927–0530).

Dining

In China, chopsticks are the utensil of choice. Be aware that the Chinese like to eat family style, with everyone sitting at a round table (which symbolizes union and perfection), burrowing their chopsticks into a common dish. It's considered bad manners to point or play with your chopsticks, or to place them on top of your rice bowl when you're finished eating (place the chopsticks horizontally on the table or plate). It is appropriate, however, to shovel rice into your mouth, to talk with your mouth full, and to stand up to reach for food across the table from you. Don't hesitate to spit bones directly onto the table: putting your fingers in your mouth is bad manners.

If you're invited to a formal Chinese meal, be prepared for great ceremony, many toasts and speeches, and a grand variety of elaborate dishes. Your host will be seated at the "head" of the round table, which is the seat that faces the door; it's differentiated from the other seats by a napkin shaped as a crown. The highest guest of honor will be seated to the host's right, the second highest guest of honor to the host's left. Don't start eating until the host takes the first bite, and then simply serve yourself as the food comes around. Be sure to **always let the food touch your plate before bringing it up to your mouth;** eating directly from the serving dish without briefly resting the food on your plate is considered bad form. It is an honor to be served by the person sitting next to you (though as a guest, you are not expected to do the same).

The restaurants we list in this book are the cream of the crop in each price category.

MEALTIMES
Lunch in China is usually served in restaurants between 11 and 2, dinner from 5 to 10. Unless otherwise noted, the restaurants listed in this guide are open daily for lunch and dinner.

Disabilities & Accessibility

There are few special facilities for people with disabilities, except in five-star hotels. Public toilets may be particularly problematic, as most are of the type you squat over, and buses, which are generally crowded, will be difficult to board. In most restaurants, museums, and other public spaces, people will be helpful and respectful to visitors with disabilities.

RESERVATIONS
When discussing accessibility with an operator or reservations agent, **ask hard questions.** Are there any stairs, inside or out? Are there grab bars next to the toilet *and* in the shower/tub? How wide is the doorway to the room? To the bathroom? For the most extensive facilities meeting the latest legal specifications, **opt for newer accommodations.**

TRAVEL AGENCIES

In the United States, the Americans with Disabilities Act requires that travel firms serve the needs of all travelers. Some agencies specialize in working with people with disabilities.

➤ **TRAVELERS WITH MOBILITY PROBLEMS: Access Adventures** (206 Chestnut Ridge Rd., Scottsville, NY 14624, tel. 716/889-9096), run by a former physical-rehabilitation counselor. **Flying Wheels Travel** (143 W. Bridge St., Box 382, Owatonna, MN 55060, tel. 507/451-5005 or 800/535-6790, fax 507/451-1685, www.flyingwheelstravel.com).

Discounts & Deals

Be a smart shopper and **compare all your options** before making decisions. A plane ticket bought with a promotional coupon from travel clubs, coupon books, and direct-mail offers or on the Internet may not be cheaper than the least expensive fare from a discount ticket agency. And always keep in mind that what you get is just as important as what you save.

DISCOUNT RESERVATIONS

To save money, **look into discount reservations services** with toll-free numbers, which use their buying power to get a better price on hotels, airline tickets, even car rentals. When booking a room, always **call the hotel's local toll-free number** (if one is available) rather than the central reservations number—you'll often get a better price. Always ask about special packages or corporate rates.

When shopping for the best deal on hotels and car rentals, **look for guaranteed exchange rates,** which protect you against a falling dollar. With your rate locked in, you won't pay more, even if the price goes up in the local currency.

➤ **HOTEL ROOMS: Players Express Vacations** (tel. 800/458-6161, www.playersexpress.com). **Steigenberger Reservation Service** (tel. 800/223-5652, www.srs-worldhotels.com). **Travel**

Interlink (tel. 800/888–5898, www.travelinterlink.com).
Turbotrip.com (tel. 800/473–7829, www.turbotrip.com).
VacationLand (tel. 800/245–0050, www.vacation-land.com).

PACKAGE DEALS

Don't confuse packages and guided tours. When you buy a package, you travel on your own, just as though you had planned the trip yourself. Fly/drive packages, which combine airfare and car rental, are often a good deal.

Electricity

To use your U.S.-purchased electric-powered equipment, **bring a converter and adapter** or buy one in the airport before you leave. The electrical current in China is 220 volts, 50 cycles alternating current (AC); wall outlets take American-style plugs, with two flat parallel prongs; however, they may not take the converter's one oversized prong, used for grounding, now in general use in the United States.

If your appliances are dual-voltage, you'll need only an adapter. Don't use 110-volt outlets marked FOR SHAVERS ONLY for high-wattage appliances such as blow-dryers. Most laptops operate equally well on 110 and 220 volts and so require only an adapter. You may also want to bring a power-surge protector.

Emergencies

If you lose your passport, contact your embassy immediately. Embassy officials can advise you on how to proceed in case of other emergencies. Your hotel may also be able to provide a translator if you need to report an emergency or crime to doctors or the police.

In a medical emergency don't call for an ambulance. The Shanghai Ambulance Service is merely a transport system. If possible, take a taxi; you'll get there faster.

AEA International 24-hour Alarm Center has information on emergency evacuations.

➤ **EMERGENCY CONTACTS: AEA International 24-hour Alarm Center** (tel. 021/6295–0099). **Ambulance Service** (tel. 120). **Fire** (tel. 119). **Police** (tel. 110).

➤ **DENTISTS: Shen Da Dental Clinic** (83–1 Taiyuan Lu, tel. 021/6437–7987). **Sino-Canadian Shanghai Dental Center** (9th People's Hospital, 639 Zhizaoju Lu, 7th floor, tel. 021/6313–3174).

➤ **HOSPITALS: Huadong Hospital** (221 Yanan Xilu, 2nd-floor Foreigners' Clinic, tel. 021/6248–3180 Ext. 6208). **Huashan Hospital** (12 Wulumuqi Lu, 19th-floor Foreigners' Clinic, tel. 021/6248–3986). **New Pioneer Medical Center** (910 Hengshan Lu, 2nd floor, tel. 6469–3898). **World Link Medical Center** (Shanghai Center, 1376 Nanjing Xilu, tel. 021/6279–7688).

English-Language Media

Foreign Languages Bookstore carries maps, photography books, and nonfiction, literature, and poetry about China, as well as foreign periodicals and a good selection of English-language novels. Along Fuzhou Lu are spanking-new bookstores like Book City, which also have small selections of English books.

➤ **BOOKSTORES: Foreign Languages Bookstore** (390 Fuzhou Lu).

Etiquette & Behavior

Be respectful and try not to get upset if things go wrong, especially when reserving tickets and hotel rooms. Be friendly but stern if you are having difficulties—raising your voice and threatening will only embarrass you in front of the Chinese, who feel that "face" is extremely important. It helps to **learn a few words of Chinese**, even if all you can say is thank you (shee-yeh shee-yeh) and hello (nee how). If you are stared at, simply smile back or treat it humorously. Playing with chopsticks is a sign of bad manners. Bowing the head and pressing the hands together is a sign of deep gratitude. Handshaking is the common greeting, but don't shake women's hands too firmly. Try to keep an open mind about anything that seems initially appalling, whether it's dog meat or Chinese toilets. The Chinese are generally a gracious people who will reciprocate kindness.

Gay & Lesbian Travel

China is still a conservative country when it comes to outward displays of affection. Although it's not unusual to see Chinese couples walking arm-in-arm in the bigger cities, Western couples, whether heterosexual or homosexual, may want to refrain from even these mild gestures. Homosexuality is not illegal but is considered a perversion or mental illness or, at the very least, improper behavior. There is a growing underground gay scene in Shanghai, but discretion is always the safest policy.

➤ GAY- & LESBIAN-FRIENDLY TRAVEL AGENCIES: Different Roads Travel (8383 Wilshire Blvd., Suite 902, Beverly Hills, CA 90211, tel. 323/651–5557 or 800/429–8747, fax 323/651–3678). Kennedy Travel (314 Jericho Turnpike, Floral Park, NY 11001, tel. 516/352–4888 or 800/237–7433, fax 516/354–8849, www.kennedytravel.com). Now Voyager (4406 18th St., San Francisco, CA 94114, tel. 415/626–1169 or 800/255–6951, fax 415/626–8626, www.nowvoyager.com). Skylink Travel and Tour (1006 Mendocino Ave., Santa Rosa, CA 95401, tel. 707/546–9888 or 800/225–5759, fax 707/546–9891, www.skylinktravel.com), serving lesbian travelers.

Health

In China you can find an English-speaking doctor in most major cities. The best place to start is with your hotel concierge, then the local Public Security Bureau. The major cities have modern hospitals, but if you become seriously ill or are injured, it is best to try to get flown home, or at least to Hong Kong, as quickly as possible. **Check for medical coverage with your health insurer before you go.**

In Hong Kong English-speaking doctors are widely available. Hotels have lists of accredited doctors and can arrange for a doctor to visit your hotel room. Otherwise, consult the nearest government hospital. Check the "Government" section of the business telephone directory under "Medical and Health Department" for a list.

Make sure you **take enough of any prescription medication for the duration of your stay.** You should also carry a copy of your prescription with you in case you lose your medicine or are stopped by customs officials. If you wear contact lenses, take a couple extra pairs along in case you lose or rip a lens. **Wear plenty of sunscreen and a good pair of sunglasses,** even during winter.

FOOD & DRINK

In China the major health risk is traveler's diarrhea, caused by eating contaminated fruit or vegetables or drinking contaminated water. So **watch what you eat.** Carry a small bottle of antibacterial hand sanitizer and wash your hands frequently. Stay away from ice, uncooked food, and unpasteurized milk and milk products, and **drink only bottled water** or water that has been boiled for at least 10 minutes. Bottled water is widely available in most major cities in China. If you're going to rural areas, bring water purification tablets. Mild cases of diarrhea may respond to Imodium (known generically as loperamide) or Pepto-Bismol (not as strong), both of which can be purchased over the counter; however, keep in mind that these may complicate more serious infections. **Do not buy prescription drugs in China** unless absolutely necessary, as the quality control is unreliable. Ask your doctor for an antidiarrheal prescription to take with you, to use in emergencies. Drink plenty of purified water or tea—chamomile is a good folk remedy—and be sure to rehydrate yourself with a salt-sugar solution (½ teaspoon salt and 4 tablespoons sugar per quart of water).

Pneumonia and influenza are also common among travelers returning from China; many health professionals recommend inoculations before you leave. Be sure you're well rested and healthy to start with.

According to the National Centers for Disease Control (CDC) there is a limited risk of hepatitis A and B, typhoid, polio, malaria, tuberculosis, dengue fever, tetanus, and rabies in small cities and rural areas. In most urban or easily accessible areas you need not worry. However, if you plan to visit remote regions or stay for more than six weeks, **check with the CDC's International Travelers Hotline.**

MEDICAL PLANS

No one plans to get sick while traveling, but it happens, so **consider signing up with a medical-assistance company.** Members get doctor referrals, emergency evacuation or repatriation, hot lines for medical consultation, cash for emergencies, and other assistance.

➤ **MEDICAL-ASSISTANCE COMPANIES: International SOS Assistance** (www.internationalsos.com; 8 Neshaminy Interplex, Suite 207, Trevose, PA 19053, tel. 215/245–4707 or 800/523–6586, fax 215/244–9617; 12 Chemin Riantbosson, 1217 Meyrin 1, Geneva, Switzerland, tel. 4122/785–6464, fax 4122/785–6424; 331 N. Bridge Rd., 17-00, Odeon Towers, Singapore 188720, tel. 65/338–7800, fax 65/338–7611).

SHOTS & MEDICATIONS

While currently no vaccinations are required to travel to China, during the summer months malaria is a serious risk in tropical and rural areas, as well as along the Yangzi River. If you'll be staying in cities for the duration of your trip, the risk of contracting malaria is small.

➤ **HEALTH WARNINGS: National Centers for Disease Control and Prevention** (CDC; National Center for Infectious Diseases, Division of Quarantine, Traveler's Health Section, 1600 Clifton Rd. NE, M/S E-03, Atlanta, GA 30333, tel. 888/232–3228 or 877/394–8747, fax 888/232–3299, www.cdc.gov).

Holidays

National holidays include January 1 (New Year's Day), two days in late February–early March (Chinese New Year, also called Spring Festival), March 8 (International Women's Day), May 1 (International Labor Day), May 4 (Youth Day), June 1 (Children's Day), July 1 (anniversary of the founding of the Communist Party of China; in Hong Kong, the anniversary of the establishment of the Special Administrative Region), August 1 (anniversary of the founding of the Chinese People's Liberation Army), and October 1 (National Day—founding of the Peoples Republic of China in 1949).

Insurance

The most useful travel-insurance plan is a comprehensive policy that includes coverage for trip cancellation and interruption, default, trip delay, and medical expenses (with a waiver for preexisting conditions).

Without insurance you will lose all or most of your money if you cancel your trip, regardless of the reason. Default insurance covers you if your tour operator, airline, or cruise line goes out of business. Trip-delay covers expenses that arise because of bad weather or mechanical delays. Study the fine print when comparing policies.

If you're traveling internationally, a key component of travel insurance is coverage for medical bills incurred if you get sick on the road. Such expenses are not generally covered by Medicare or private policies. U.K. residents can buy a travel-insurance policy valid for most vacations taken during the year in which it's purchased (but check preexisting-condition coverage).

Always **buy travel policies directly from the insurance company**; if you buy them from a cruise line, airline, or tour operator that goes out of business you probably will not be covered for the agency or operator's default, a major risk. Before making any purchase, **review your existing health and home-owner's policies** to find what they cover away from home.

➤ **TRAVEL INSURERS: In the U.S.: Access America** (6600 W. Broad St., Richmond, VA 23230, tel. 800/284–8300, fax 804/673–1491, www.etravelprotection.com), **Travel Guard International** (1145 Clark St., Stevens Point, WI 54481, tel. 715/345–0505 or 800/826–1300, fax 800/955–8785, www.noelgroup.com).

➤ **INSURANCE INFORMATION: In the U.K.: Association of British Insurers** (51–55 Gresham St., London EC2V 7HQ, U.K., tel. 020/7600–3333, fax 020/7696–8999, www.abi.org.uk). In Canada: **RBC Travel Insurance** (6880 Financial Dr., Mississauga, Ontario L5N 7Y5, Canada, tel. 905/791–8700, 800/668–4342 in Canada, fax 905/816–2498, www.royalbank.com). In Australia: **Insurance Council of Australia** (Level 3, 56 Pitt St., Sydney NSW 2000, tel. 02/9253–5100, fax 02/9253–5111, www.ica.com.au). In New Zealand: **Insurance Council of New Zealand** (Box 474, Wellington, New Zealand, tel. 04/472–5230, fax 04/473–3011, www.icnz.org.nz).

Internet

Although the Internet (*īntèrlái* in pinyin) is still a novel concept for most Chinese outside of metropolitan areas, cybercafés and other types of computer centers are quickly spreading, especially in the large cities. Due to government restrictions, many Chinese still find browsing limited, but many professional Chinese these days do have E-mail addresses. Most major hotels in China have access to the Internet through their business centers, and some even allow you to use it from your room, provided your computer is equipped with the proper tools (modem, 220-volt adapter, Web browser, etc.) Be prepared for very slow dial-ups, and inquire about cost in cybercafés before going on-line. Consider signing up for a free Internet-based E-mail account before you go.

Language

The national language of China is Mandarin, known in China as Putonghua (*pǔtōnghuà*), "common language." Nearly everyone speaks Mandarin, but many also speak local dialects, some of which use the same characters as Mandarin with a very different pronunciation.

All of the Chinese languages are tonal; there are four possible tones for every syllable, in addition to the basic sound of the syllable, and they make up part of a word's pronunciation. Each syllable has a different meaning depending on the pitch or musical inflection the speaker gives it. For example, in Mandarin the syllable *ma* can mean mother, horse, curse, or hemp plant—or, it can be a particle denoting a question—depending on the tone used. Thus, the sentence "Ma ma ma ma" translates as "does mother curse the horse?," a classic example of the complexity of the tonal Chinese language.

Additionally, many Chinese characters are *homonyms*, which makes it difficult if not impossible for the foreign ear to understand what is being said. Since 1949 the government has revamped the teaching of Mandarin, introducing a simplified phonetic system known as pinyin, which uses the Roman alphabet to denote the pronunciations of the myriad Chinese characters (pinyin is taught alongside, and not instead of, ideograms). Names of sites in this book are given in pinyin with English translations, and lists of Chinese place names in the chapters provide the names of recommended sites in Chinese characters.

Although Chinese grammar is simple, it is still difficult for foreigners to speak Chinese and even harder to be understood. However, the Chinese will appreciate your making the effort to speak a few phrases understood almost everywhere. Try "Hello"—"Ní hǎo" (nee how); "Thank you"—"Xiè xiè" (shee-yeh, shee-yeh); and "Good-bye"—"Zai jian" (dzigh djyan). When pronouncing words written in pinyin, remember that "q" and "x" are pronounced like "ch" and "sh," respectively; "zh" is pronounced like the "j" in "just"; "c" is pronounced like "ts".

You can usually find someone who speaks English in the major cities. Fortunately, almost all cities have street signs written in pinyin. It can be difficult to get around China on your own without speaking the language. If you are not planning to go with a tour group, you can go from city to city and hire a local English-speaking guide from the CTS office at each stop.

➤ **LANGUAGE RESOURCE:** *I Can Read That! A Traveler's Introduction to Chinese Characters,* by Julie Mazel Sussman, China Books and Periodicals, Inc. (tel. 415/282–2994, fax 415/282–0994, www.chinabooks.com). *In the Know in China,* by Jennifer Phillips, Living Language/Random House Inc. (tel. 800/726–0600, www.livinglanguage.com). **Business Companion: Chinese,** by Tim Dobbins and Paul Westbrook, Living Language/Random House Inc. (tel. 800/726–0600, www.livinglanguage.com).

Lodging

The lodgings we list are the cream of the crop in each price category. We always list the facilities that are available—but we don't specify whether they cost extra: when pricing accommodations, always ask what's included and what costs extra. Also be aware that price may have little bearing on quality in China.

HOTELS

Always **bring your passport when checking into a hotel.** The reception desk clerk will have to see it and record the number before you can be given a room. Sometimes unmarried couples are not allowed to stay together in the same room, but simply wearing a band on your left finger is one way to avoid this complication. Friends of the same sex, especially women, shouldn't have a problem getting a room together. There may, however, be regulations about who is allowed in your room, and it's also normal for hotels to post "visitor hours" inside the room.

All hotels listed have private bath unless otherwise noted. Remember that water is a precious resource in China and use accordingly.

Mail & Shipping

Post offices are open from 8 AM to 6 PM Monday through Saturday. Public post offices are generally crowded, but large hotels have postal services open all day Monday through Saturday and Sunday 8 to noon.

POSTAL RATES

A postcard to the United States costs Y4.2. A letter, up to 20 grams, costs Y5.40.

RECEIVING MAIL

Long-term guests can receive mail at their hotels. Otherwise, the best place to receive mail is at the American Express office. Most major Chinese cities have American Express offices with client mail service. Be sure to bring your American Express card, as the staff will not give you the mail without seeing it.

Money Matters

Standard museum entrance fees range between Y20 and Y50 and vary according to whether you're a local or a foreigner. A soft drink costs about Y10. A dumpling costs about Y10; a slice of pizza costs about Y50. Newspapers are about Y20; the *Herald Tribune*, printed in Hong Kong, is Y30. Prices throughout this guide are given for adults. Substantially reduced fees are almost always available for children, students, and senior citizens.

ATMS

ATMs using the Cirrus and Plus networks are increasingly common in larger cities throughout China; at last count there were nearly 50 in Shanghai.

Before leaving home, **make sure your credit cards have been programmed for ATM use in China.** Local bank cards often do not work overseas or may access only your checking account; **ask your bank about a MasterCard/Cirrus or Visa debit card,** which works like a bank card but can be used at any ATM displaying a MasterCard/Cirrus or Visa logo. These cards, too, may tap only your checking account; check with your bank about their policy.

CREDIT CARDS

Upscale hotels and restaurants, travel agencies such as CITS, tourist shops, and shopping centers will usually accept American Express, MasterCard, and Visa. Credit cards are less commonly accepted outside cities. Contact your credit card company before you go to inform them of your trip. Credit card companies have been known to put a hold on an account and send a report to their fraud division upon registering a purchase or cash advance in China. Be sure to copy your credit card numbers on a separate piece of paper and carry it in a place separate from your credit cards in case of theft.

Throughout this guide, the following abbreviations are used: **AE,** American Express; **DC,** Diner's Club; **MC,** MasterCard; and **V,** Visa.

➤ **REPORTING LOST CARDS: American Express** (tel. 202/ 554–2639). **Diner's Club** (tel. 303/799–1504 in the U.S.).

MasterCard (tel. 010/800–110–7309 in China).**Visa** (tel. 010/800–110–2911 in China).

CURRENCY

The Chinese currency is officially called the renminbi (RMB), or "People's Money." You can change money at most Bank of China branches, at the front desk of most upscale hotels, or at international airports. **Carry currency in several forms** (and in several different places) while abroad, such as cash, traveler's checks, and an ATM and/or credit card.

The Bank of China issues RMB bills in denominations of 2, 5, 10, 50, 100, 500, and 1,000 yuan. Yuan are commonly referred to as kuài (kwye); the abbreviation is Y. The exchange rates are approximately Y8.28 = $1 US, Y5.59 = 1C$, Y4.44 = 1$ Australian, Y11.96 = £1, Y3.71 = 1$ New Zealand, Y9.9 = 1 Irish punt, and Y1.1 = 1 South African rand.

CURRENCY EXCHANGE

For the most favorable rates, **change money through banks.** Although ATM transaction fees may be higher abroad than at home, ATM rates are excellent because they are based on wholesale rates offered only by major banks. You won't do as well at exchange booths in airports or rail and bus stations, in hotels, in restaurants, or in stores. Generally speaking, you'll get a better deal when you exchange money within China, but do **purchase a small amount of renminbi prior to your trip.**

➤ **EXCHANGE SERVICES: International Currency Express** (tel. 888/278–6628 for orders, www.foreignmoney.com). **Thomas Cook Currency Services** (tel. 800/287–7362 for telephone orders and retail locations, www.us.thomascook.com).

TRAVELER'S CHECKS

Even though there is an increasing number of ATMs in China, your best bet is to take traveler's checks. **Take cash or exchange money in larger cities first if your trip includes rural areas** and small towns; take traveler's checks to cities. Lost or stolen checks can usually be replaced within 24 hours. To ensure a speedy refund, buy your own traveler's checks—don't let someone else pay for them: irregularities like this can cause delays. Be sure to keep your traveler's check receipts in a different place from your traveler's checks.

Packing

Although the Chinese have become more fashion-conscious in the past few years, informal attire is still appropriate for most occasions. The streets are dirty, so you may prefer to bring older clothes and shoes. Sturdy, comfortable walking shoes are a must. A raincoat, especially a light Goretex one or a fold-up poncho, is useful for an onset of rainy weather. Summers are very hot and winters very cold in most of China, so pack accordingly. Avoid bringing clothes that need dry-cleaning. You will find it much easier to get around if you travel light, with no more than two or three changes of clothes, so bring clothes that you can layer should you need extra warmth. Clothes are also inexpensive in China, so you can always buy what you need. Most hotels have reliable overnight laundry, mending, and pressing services, so you can have your clothes washed frequently.

Be sure to pack the following essentials: alarm clock, contraceptives, dental floss, deodorant, mosquito repellent, shampoo, shaving cream and razors, sunglasses, sunscreen, tampons, toothbrush, and toothpaste. High-end hotels will generally provide a hair drier in the room.

If you're planning a longer trip or will be using local tour guides, bring a few inexpensive items from your home country as gifts. American cigarettes are popular in China, but if you don't wish to promote smoking, bring candy, T-shirts, or small cosmetic items, such as lipstick and nail polish. **Do not give American magazines and books as gifts,** as this could be considered propaganda and get your Chinese friends into trouble.

In your carry-on luggage, **pack an extra pair of eyeglasses or contact lenses and enough of any medication** you take to last the entire trip. You may also ask your doctor to write a spare prescription using the drug's generic name, since brand names may vary from country to country. In luggage to be checked, **never pack prescription drugs or valuables.** To avoid customs and security delays, carry medications in their original packaging. **Don't pack any sharp objects** in your carry-on luggage, including knives of any size or material, scissors, manicure tools, and corkscrews, or anything else that might arouse suspicion.

CHECKING LUGGAGE

You are allowed one carry-on bag and one personal article, such as a purse or a laptop computer. Make sure that everything you carry aboard will fit under your seat or in the overhead bin. Get to the gate early, so you can board as soon as possible, before the overhead bins fill up. Be sure to lock your bags, both for safety reasons and because some local carriers require that all bags be locked before they can be checked.

If you are flying internationally, note that baggage allowances may be determined not by piece but by weight—generally 88 pounds (40 kilograms) in first class, 66 pounds (30 kilograms) in business class, and 44 pounds (20 kilograms) in economy.

Airline liability for baggage is limited to $1,250 per person on flights within the United States. On international flights it amounts to $9.07 per pound or $20 per kilogram for checked baggage (roughly $640 per 70-pound bag) and $400 per passenger for unchecked baggage. You can buy additional coverage at check-in for about $10 per $1,000 of coverage, but it excludes a rather extensive list of items, shown on your airline ticket.

Before departure, **itemize your bags' contents** and their worth, and label the bags with your name, address, and phone number.

(If you use your home address, cover it so potential thieves can't see it readily.) Inside each bag, **pack a copy of your itinerary**. At check-in, **make sure that each bag is correctly tagged with the** destination airport's three-letter code. If your bags arrive damaged or fail to arrive at all, file a written report with the airline before leaving the airport.

Passports & Visas

When traveling internationally, **carry your passport** even if you don't need one (it's always the best form of I.D.) and **make two photocopies of the data page** (one for someone at home and another for you, carried separately from your passport). If you lose your passport, promptly call the nearest embassy or consulate and the local police.

ENTERING CHINA

All U.S. citizens, even infants, need a valid passport with a tourist visa stamped in it to enter China for stays of up to 90 days.

GETTING A VISA

It takes about a week to get a visa in the United States. Costs range from about $35 for a visa issued within two working days to $50 for a visa issued overnight. **Note:** The visa application will ask your occupation. The Chinese do not like journalists or anyone who works in publishing or media. Americans and Canadians in these professions routinely state "teacher" under "Occupation." U.K. passports state the bearer's occupation, and this can be problematic for anyone in the "wrong" line of work. Several years ago a British journalist on holiday in Beijing was detained for a day because of his occupation. Before you go, contact the consulate of the People's Republic of China to see how strict the current mood is.

To extend your visa or ask for information about your status as an alien in China, stop by the Public Security Bureau Division for Aliens—it's open weekdays 9–11 and 2–5. The office is extremely bureaucratic, and the visa officers can be difficult. Most of them can speak English. It's usually no problem to get a month's extension on a tourist visa. You'll need to bring in your passport and your registration of temporary residency from the hotel at which you're staying. If you are trying to extend a business visa, you'll need the above items as well as a letter from the business that originally invited you to China saying it would like to extend your stay for work reasons. Rules are always changing, so you will probably need to go to the office at least twice to get all your papers in order.

➤ **CONTACTS: Public Security Bureau Division for Aliens** (333 Wusong Lu, tel. 021/6357–6666).

➤ **IN AUSTRALIA: Chinese Embassy** (tel. 02/6273–4780 Ext. 218 and 258, fax 02/6273–9615, www.chinaembassy.org.au).

➤ **IN CANADA: Chinese Embassy** (tel. 613/789–3434, fax 613/789–1911, www.chinaembassycanada.org).

➤ **IN NEW ZEALAND: Chinese Embassy** (tel. 04/472–1382, fax 04/499–0419, www.chinaembassy.org.nz).

➤ **IN THE U.K.: Chinese Embassy** (tel. 0171/636–2580, fax 0171/636–2981, www.chinese-embassy.org.uk).

➤ **IN THE U.S.: Chinese Embassy** (Room 110, 2201 Wisconsin Ave. NW, Washington, DC 20007, tel. 202/338–6688, fax 202/588–9760, www.china-embassy.org). **Chinese Consulate** (Visa Office, 520 12th Ave., New York, NY 10036; tel. 212/736–9301, automatic answering machine with 24-hour service; 212/502–0271, information desk open weekdays 2–4, fax 212/502–0245, www.nyconsulate.prchina.org).

PASSPORT OFFICES
The best time to apply for a passport or to renew is in fall and winter. Before any trip, check your passport's expiration date, and, if necessary, renew it as soon as possible.

➤ **AUSTRALIAN CITIZENS: Australian Passport Office** (tel. 131–232, www.dfat.gov.au/passports).

➤ **CANADIAN CITIZENS: Passport Office** (tel. 819/994–3500; 800/567–6868 in Canada, www.dfait-maeci.gc.ca/passport).

➤ **NEW ZEALAND CITIZENS: New Zealand Passport Office** (tel. 04/494–0700, www.passports.govt.nz).

➤ **U.K. CITIZENS: London Passport Office** (tel. 0870/521–0410, www.ukpa.gov.uk) for fees and documentation requirements and to request an emergency passport.

➤ **U.S. CITIZENS: National Passport Information Center** (tel. 900/225–5674; calls are 35¢ per minute for automated service, $1.05 per minute for operator service; www.travel.state.gov/npicinfo.html).

Rest Rooms

Hotels, restaurants, and boats that often accommodate foreigners are usually equipped with Western toilets, but you are likely to encounter the standard model—squat toilets with or without a flush feature—in airports, train stations, trains, schools, parks, and other public spaces. Some cities' sanitation systems cannot handle toilet paper, and a wastebasket is provided for disposal. Be sure to carry toilet paper with you at all times, especially if you're taking a train or heading to the countryside. Moist towelettes are also invaluable.

Safety

There is little violent crime against tourists in China, partly because the penalties are severe for those who are caught—execution is the most common. Use the lock-box in your hotel room to store any valuables, but always carry your passport with you for identification purposes.

The traffic in Chinese cities is usually heavy and just as out of control as it looks. Be very careful when crossing streets or riding a bicycle.

Respiratory problems may be aggravated by the severely polluted air in China's cities. Some residents as well as visitors find that wearing a surgical mask, or a scarf or bandana, helps.

LOCAL SCAMS

Pickpocketing is a growing problem. Keep valuables in a money belt or locked in a hotel safe. A general rule of thumb is **don't wear anything that will stand out,** that is, revealing or flashy clothes or expensive jewelry. If nothing else, you may be harassed by people politely asking if you will trade clothes or give them your watch!

Senior-Citizen Travel

To qualify for age-related discounts, **mention your senior-citizen status up front** when booking hotel reservations (not when checking out) and before you're seated in restaurants (not when paying the bill). When renting a car, ask about promotional car-rental discounts, which can be cheaper than senior-citizen rates.

➤ **EDUCATIONAL PROGRAMS: Elderhostel** (11 Ave. de Lafayette, Boston, MA 02111-1746, tel. 877/426–8056, fax 877/426–2166, www.elderhostel.org). **Folkways Institute** (14600 S.E. Aldridge Rd., Portland, OR 97236-6518, tel. 503/658–6600 or 800/225–4666, fax 503/658–8672, www.folkwaystravel.com).

Subway Travel

Still under construction, the Shanghai Metro is constantly being expanded. So far, two lines are functional, with a third in trial operation. Eight more lines are in the works, to be completed over the next two decades. With Shanghai's traffic-choked streets, it is by far the quickest way to get to most places. Line one travels between Xinzhuang and the Shanghai Railway Station, with stops in the French Concession at Changshu Lu, Shaanxi Lu, and Huangpi Lu. The second line, which will eventually link Hongqiao Airport with Pudong airport, currently runs from Zhongshan Gongyuan to Zhangjiang Station in Pudong.

The subway is not too crowded except at rush hour, and trains run regularly. Service begins just before 5 AM and ends at about 10:45, depending upon the line you are taking. Tickets cost Y2–Y5 with no charge for changing trains.

Taxes

There is no sales tax in China. Hotels have a room tariff of 10% for service charges plus 5% tax. Airport departure tax is Y90 (about $11), payable in yuan only. Domestic flights require a Y50 ($6) airport construction fee, cash only.

Taxis

By far the most comfortable way to get around Shanghai, taxis are plentiful and easy to spot. Most are red Volkswagen Santanas, although they also come in white, green, yellow, and blue. They are all metered. You can spot the available ones by the red FOR HIRE sign in the window on the passenger side. The fare starts at Y12, with each km (½ mi) thereafter costing Y2. After 10 km (6 mi), the price per kilometer goes up to Y2.70. You also pay for waiting time in traffic.

Cabs can be hailed on the street or called for by phone. Most cab drivers don't speak English, so it's best to give them a piece of paper with your destination written in Chinese (keep a card or piece of paper with the name of your hotel on it handy for the return trip). Hotel doormen can also help you tell the driver where you're going. It's a good idea to study a map and have some idea where you are, as many drivers will take you for a ride—a much longer one—if they think they can get away with it.

➤ **TAXI COMPANIES: Dazhong Taxi Company** (tel. 021/6258–1688). **Friendship Taxi Company** (tel. 021/6258–3484). **Shanghai Taxi Company** (tel. 021/6258–0000).

Telephones

AREA & COUNTRY CODES
The country code for China is 86; the city code for Shanghai is 21. When dialing from within the country, add 0 before the city code. The country code is 1 for the United States and Canada, 61 for Australia, 64 for New Zealand, and 44 for the United Kingdom.

To dial overseas direct, the international access code is 001.

DIRECTORY & OPERATOR ASSISTANCE
It's hard to find English-speaking operators in China, except through international directory assistance (dial 115). You can dial overseas direct from many hotel room and business center telephones. The international access code in China is 00. Hotels usually add a 30% surcharge to long-distance calls.

Local directory assistance, tel. 114 (Shanghai). Domestic directory assistance, tel. 116 (other Chinese cities). Time, tel. 117. Weather, tel. 121.

LONG-DISTANCE SERVICES
AT&T, MCI, and Sprint access codes make calling long distance relatively convenient, but you may find the local access number blocked in many hotel rooms. First ask the hotel operator to connect you. If the hotel operator balks, ask for an international operator, or dial the international operator yourself. One way to improve your odds of getting connected to your long-distance carrier is to travel with more than one company's calling card (a

hotel may block Sprint, for example, but not MCI). If all else fails, call from a pay phone.

Most major hotels now have International Direct Dial (IDD) phones.

The local access code in China is 11 for AT&T, 12 for MCI, and 13 for Sprint—dial these numbers after dialing the local operator (108), who will speak English.

➤ **ACCESS CODES: AT&T Direct** (tel. 800/874–4000). **MCI WorldPhone** (tel. 800/444–4444). **Sprint International Access** (tel. 800/793–1153).

PUBLIC PHONES

Most hotels have phone booths where you can place domestic and international calls. You pay a deposit of about Y200 and receive a card with the number of the phone booth. A computer times the call and processes a bill, which you pay at the end. Post offices have telecommunications centers where you can buy cards in denominations of Y20, Y50, and Y100 to make long-distance calls. Standard pay phones accept these cards, as well as coins. The cards tend to be less expensive but only work in the province in which they were purchased.

Tipping

Because the Chinese Government forbids asking for tips, tipping used to be unheard of, but now the custom is taking hold in hotels and restaurants. It's not necessary to tip taxi drivers, although you might let them keep small change.

CTS tour guides are not allowed to accept tips. You can **give guides and drivers small gifts.** They often appreciate American cigarettes, but you also can offer American candy or T-shirts. If you hire a driver and guide independently, the tipping norm is $10 per day for the guide and $5 per day for the driver.

Tours & Packages

Because everything is prearranged on a prepackaged tour or independent vacation, you spend less time planning—and often get it all at a good price.

BOOKING WITH AN AGENT

Travel agents are excellent resources. But it's a good idea to collect brochures from several agencies as some agents' suggestions may be influenced by relationships with tour and package firms that reward them for volume sales. If you have a special interest, **find an agent with expertise in that area;** ASTA (☞ Travel Agencies) has a database of specialists worldwide.

Make sure your travel agent knows the accommodations and other services of the place being recommended. Ask about the hotel's location, room size, beds, and whether it has a pool, room service, or programs for children, if you care about these. Has your agent been there in person or sent others whom you can contact?

Do some homework on your own, too: local tourism boards can provide information about lesser-known and small-niche operators, some of which may sell only direct.

BUYER BEWARE

Each year consumers are stranded or lose their money when tour operators—even large ones with excellent reputations—go out of business. So **check out the operator.** Ask several travel agents about its reputation, and try to **book with a company that has a consumer-protection program.** (Look for information in the company's brochure.) In the United States, members of the National Tour Association and the United States Tour Operators Association are required to set aside funds to cover your payments and travel arrangements in the event that the company defaults. It's also a good idea to choose a company that participates in the American Society of Travel Agents' Tour

Operator Program (TOP); ASTA will act as mediator in any disputes between you and your tour operator.

Remember that the more your package or tour includes the better you can predict the ultimate cost of your vacation. Make sure you know exactly what is covered, and **beware of hidden costs.** Are taxes, tips, and transfers included? Entertainment and excursions? These can add up.

➤ **TOUR-OPERATOR RECOMMENDATIONS: American Society of Travel Agents** (☞ Travel Agencies). **Cameron Tours** (6249 N. Kingston St., McLean, VA 22101, tel. 703/538–7122 or 800/648–4635, www.camerontours.com). **Chn–Asia Express Tours** (22 Main St., South River, NJ 08882, tel. 732/432–7569, fax 732/432–7545). **Imperial Tours** 1802 N. Carson St., Suite 212–2296, Carson City, NV 89701, tel. 888/296–5306, fax 800/380–6576, www.imperialtours.net). **National Tour Association** (NTA; 546 E. Main St., Lexington, KY 40508, tel. 859/226–4444 or 800/682–8886, www.ntaonline.com). **United States Tour Operators Association** (USTOA; 342 Madison Ave., Suite 1522, New York, NY 10173, tel. 212/599–6599 or 800/468–7862, fax 212/599–6744, www.ustoa.com).

Train Travel

Shanghai is connected to many destinations in China by direct train. The Shanghai Railway Station 24-hr train information) is in the northern part of the city. Several trains a day run to Suzhou, Hangzhou, Nanjing, and other nearby destinations. The best train to catch to Beijing is the overnight express that leaves around 7 PM and arrives in Beijing the next morning. An express train also runs to Hong Kong.

You can buy train tickets at CITS, but a service fee is charged. Same-day, next-day, and sometimes third-day tickets can also be easily purchased at the ticket office in the Longmen Hotel, on the western side of the train station.

Train tickets usually have to be purchased in the city of origin. If you do not speak Mandarin, it will be difficult to negotiate the ticket windows at the train station even though there is a special ticket counter just for foreigners, so buy tickets from the local CTS office or ask your hotel concierge to make the arrangements. Fares are more expensive for foreigners than for the Chinese. Make train reservations at least a day or two in advance, if you can. Boiled water is always available.

Trains are always crowded, so arrive at the station two hours before departure.

➤ **TRAIN INFORMATION: Shanghai Railway Station** (303 Moling Lu, tel. 021/6317–9090). **Ticket office** (777 Hengfeng Lu, tel. 021/6317–0000).

CLASSES

Although China's classless society has all but disappeared, the train system offers a glimpse of old-fashioned socialist euphemisms. Instead of first-class and second-class accommodations, passengers choose hard seat or soft seat, and for overnight journeys, hard sleeper or soft sleeper. The soft sleeper has four compartments with soft beds and is recommended if you're taking a long journey (though it is much more expensive than the hard sleeper). You should note, however, that theft on trains is increasingly common; on overnight trains, be sure to sleep with your valuables or else keep them on the inside of the bunk.

Travel Agencies

A good travel agent puts your needs first. Look for an agency that has been in business at least five years, emphasizes customer service, and has someone on staff who specializes in your destination. In addition, **make sure the agency belongs to a professional trade organization.** The American Society of Travel Agents (ASTA), with more than 26,000 members in some 170 countries, is the largest and most influential in the field. Operating under the motto "Without a travel agent, you're on your own," it maintains and enforces a strict code of ethics and will step in to help mediate any agent-client disputes if necessary. ASTA also maintains a Web site that includes a directory of agents. (If a travel agency is also acting as your tour operator, *see* Buyer Beware in Tours & Packages.)

➤ **LOCAL AGENT REFERRALS: American Express** (Shanghai Center, 1376 Nanjing Xilu, tel. 021/6279–8600). **China International Travel Service** (CITS; Guangming Bldg., 2 Jinling Lu, tel. 021/6321–7200). **Evrokantakt** (9T Tseng Chow Commercial Mansion, 1590 Yanan Xilu, tel. 021/6280–9579). **Harvest Travel Services** (16–A6 Harvest Bldg., 585 Longhua Xilu, tel. 021/6469–1860). **IRS International Travel Agency** (tel. 021/6486–0681 or 021/6486–0682). **Jebsen and Co. Ltd.** (16 Henan Lu, tel. 021/6355–4001).

Visitor Information

For general information before you go, including information about tours, insurance, and safety, call or visit the National Tourist Office in New York City, Los Angeles, London, or Sydney.

Within China, China International Travel Service (CITS) and China Travel Service (CTS) are under the same government ministry. Local offices, catering to sightseeing around the area (and to visitors from other mainland cities), are called CTS. CITS offices can book international flights.

➤ **CHINA NATIONAL TOURIST OFFICES: Australia** (19th floor, 44 Market St., Sydney, NSW 2000, tel. 02/9299–4057, fax 02/9290–1958, www.cnto.org.au). **Canada** (556 W. Broadway, Vancouver, BC V5Z 1E9, tel. 604/872–8787, fax 604/873–2823, www.citscanada.com.) **United Kingdom** 4 Glentworth St., London NW1, tel. 0171/935–9427, fax 0171/487–5842). **United States** (350 5th Ave., Suite 6413, New York, NY 10118, 212/760–8218, fax

212/760–8809; 333 W. Broadway, Suite 201, Glendale, CA 91204, tel. 818/545–7504, fax 818/545–7506, www.cnto.org).

➤ **CHINA INTERNATIONAL TRAVEL SERVICE (CITS): United States** (2 Mott St., New York, NY 10002, tel. 212/608–1212 or 800/899–8618).

➤ **IN SHANGHAI: Shanghai Tourist Information Services** (Hongqiao Airport, tel. 021/6268–7788 ext. 6750; People's Square Metro Station, tel. 021/6438–1693; Yuyuan Commercial Building, tel. 021/6355–4909). **Spring Travel Service,** tel. 021/6252–0000 ext. 0). **Tourist Hotline** (tel. 021/6439–0630).

➤ **U.S. GOVERNMENT ADVISORIES: U.S. Department of State** (Overseas Citizens Services Office, Room 4811 N.S., 2201 C St. NW, Washington, DC 20520, tel. 202/647–5225 for interactive hot line, www.travel.state.gov); enclose a self-addressed, stamped, business-size envelope.

Web Sites

Do check out the World Wide Web when planning your trip. You'll find everything from weather forecasts to virtual tours of famous cities. Be sure to **visit Fodors.com** (www.fodors.com), a complete travel-planning site. You can research prices and book plane tickets, hotel rooms, rental cars, vacation packages, and more.

The government and regional tourist agencies in China sponsor a number of Web sites that can be accessed from the United States. Try www.chinatips.net, www.yahoo.com/cn, www.travelchinaguide.com, www.china.com, www.chinavista.com, www.english.ccnt.com.cn, and www.china.pages.com.cn.

The China National Tourism Office is at www.cnto.org. You can also visit CITS at www.chinatravelservice.com or www.citsusa.com.

When to Go

Summer is the peak tourist season, and hotels and transportation can be very crowded. Book early—several months in advance if possible—for summer travel. The weather can be scorching in the summer in most of China. The weather will be better and the crowds not quite as dense in late spring and early fall, although then you need to be prepared for rain. Winter is bitterly cold and not conducive to travel in most of the country. Avoid traveling around Chinese New Year, as much of China shuts down and the Chinese themselves travel, making reservations into and out of China virtually impossible to get.

➤ **FORECASTS: Weather Channel Connection** (tel. 900/932–8437), 95¢ per minute from a Touch-Tone phone.

What follows are average daily maximum and minimum temperatures in Shanghai.

SHANGHAI

Jan.	46F	8C	May	77F	25C	Sept.	82F	28C
	33	1		59	15		66	19
Feb.	47F	8C	June	82F	28C	Oct.	74F	23C
	34	1		67	19		57	14
Mar.	55F	13C	July	90F	32C	Nov.	63F	17C
	40	4		74	23		45	7
Apr.	66F	19C	Aug.	90F	32C	Dec.	53F	12C
	50	10		74	23		36	2

CHINESE PLACE NAMES

SHANGHAI

Pinyin	English	Chinese Character
Chén Xiàng Gé	Chen Ziang Ge	陈香阁
Dàjìng Gé	Old City Wall	大境路老城墙
Dōngtái Lù Gudài Chǎng	Dongtai Road Antiques Market	东台路古代场
Shànghǎi Pǔdōng Fázhǎn Yínháng	Former Hongkong & Shanghai Bank	上海浦东发展银行
Fúyóu Lù Gudài Chǎng	Fuyou Road Antiques Market	富有路古代场
Hǎiguān Lóu	Customs House	海关楼
Hépíng Fàndiàn	Peace Hotel	和平饭店
Huángpu Gōngyuán	Huangpu Park	黄埔公园
Wài Tān	The Bund	外滩
Yùyuán	Yu Garden	豫园
Húxīntīng Cháshì	Midlake Pavilion Teahouse	湖心亭茶室
Zhōngguo Yínháng	Bank of China	中国银行
Dà Jù Yuàn	Grand Theatre	上海大剧院
Dà Shìjiè	Great World	大世界
Guójì Fàndiàn	Park Hotel	国际饭店
Huā Niǎo Shìchǎng	Bird and Flower Market	花鸟市场
Jìngān Gu Sì	Jingan Temple	静安古寺
Rénmín Gōngyuán	People's Park	人民公园
Rénmín Guǎng Chǎng	People's Square	人民广场
Shànghǎi Bówùguǎn	Shanghai Museum	上海博物馆
Shànghǎi Měishùguǎn	Shanghai Art Museum	上海美术馆
Shànghǎi Zhánlán Zhōngxīn	Shanghai Exhibition Center	上海展览中心
Yúfó Sì	Jade Buddha Temple	玉佛寺

Fúxīng Gōngyuán	Fuxing Park	复兴公园
Lónghuá Gu Sì	Longhua Temple	龙华古寺
Lánxīn	Lyceum Theatre	兰心大剧院
Shànghǎi Gōngyì Měishù Yànjiūsuǒ	Shanghai Arts and Crafts Research Institute	上海工艺美术研究所
Sóng Qìnglíng Gùjū	Soong Chingling's Former Residence	宋庆龄故居
Sūn Zhōngshān Gùjū	Song Yat-sen's Former Residence	孙中山故居
Yàndàng Lù	Yandan Lu Pedestrian Street	雁荡路
Xújiāhuì Dàjiàotáng	Xujiahui Cathedral	徐家汇教堂
Zhōnggòng Yīdàhuìzhi	Site of the First National Congress	中共一大会址
Bīngjiāng Dà Dào	Riverside Promenade	冰江大道
Dōngfāng Míngzhū	Oriental Pearl TV Tower	东方明珠
Jīnmào Dàshà	Jinmao Building	金茂大厦
Pǔdōng Mǎtóu	Pudong Ferry Terminal	浦东码头
Shànghǎi Lìshǐ Bówùguǎn	Shanghai History Museum	上海历史博物馆
Shànghǎi Zhèngquàn Jiāoyìsuo	Shanghai Securities Exchange Building	上海证券交易所
Lu Xùn Gōngyuán	Lu Xun Park	鲁迅公园
Móxī Huìtáng	Moshe Synagogue	摩西会堂
Huǒshān Gōngyuán	Huoshan Park	火山公园

EASTERN CHINA

Pinyin	English	Chinese Character
Jiāngsū	Jiangsu	江苏
Nánjīng	Nanjing	南京
Sūzhōu	Suzhou	苏州
Wúxī	Wuxi	无锡
Zhènjiāng	Zhenjiang	镇江
Huángshān	Huangshan	黄山

CHINESE VOCABULARY

Many of the pronunciations for the *pinyin* below appear to have two syllables. Actually, there are two separate sounds, but they move smoothly from one into the other and make but a single sound when said correctly. For example, the *pinyin* "dian" is pronounced "dee-**en**," with a slight emphasis on the second part of the word: this should be a single sound, as opposed to what you would hear if you said separately the letters "D" and "N." Below, only the words with hyphens in them are pronounced this way. All other "spelled sounds" (a literal translation of the word *pinyin*) should be pronounced as indicated.

English	Pinyin	Pronunciation
BASICS		
Yes/there is/to have	yǒu	yoh
No/there isn't/ to not have	méi yǒu	**may** yoh
Please	qǐng	ching
Thank you	xìe xìe	**shay** shay
Excuse me	má fan nǐ	mah fahn nee
Sorry	duì bù qǐ	**dway** boo chee
Good/bad	hǎo/bù hǎo	how/**boo** how
Goodbye	zài jiàn	dzy jee-**en** (y as in why)
Mr. (Sir)	xiānshēng	shee-**en** shung
Mrs. (Ma'am)	fū rén	**nyoo** shuh
Miss	xiǎo jiě	shee-**ao** jee-**ay**

DAYS OF THE WEEK, TIME EXPRESSIONS

Sunday	xīng qī rì/	shing chee dz/
	xīng qī tiān	shing chee tee-en
Monday	xīng qī yī	shing chee ee
Tuesday	xīng qī èr	shing chee **ahr**
Wednesday	xīng qī sān	shing chee **sahn**
Thursday	xīng qī sì	shing chee **sih**
Friday	xīng qī wǔ	shing chee **woo**
Saturday	xīng qī lìu	shing chee **lee-o**
Week	xīng qī	shing chee
Month/moon	yuè	yway
Year	nián	nee-en
When	shén me shí hóu?	shun muh shur ho?
Night/evening	wǎn shàng	wahn **shahng**
Yesterday	zuó tiān	zwo tee-en
Today	jīn tiān	jeen tee-**en**
Tomorrow	míng tiān	ming tee-**en**

NUMBERS

1	yī	ee
2	èr (used as a numeral)	ahr
2 of . . .	liǎng	lee-**ahng**
3	sān	sahn
4	sì	sih
5	wǔ	woo
6	lìu	**lee**-o
7	qì	chee
8	bā	bah
9	jǐu	jee-**o**
10	shí	shur
11	shí yī (10 + 1)	shur **ee**
15	shí wǔ	**shur** woo
20	èr shí (2 x 10)	**ahr** shur

21	èr shí yī (2 x 10 + 1)	**ahr** shur **ee**
30	sān shí	**sahn** shur
50	wǔ shí	woo shur
100	(yī) bǎi	(ee) by
200	èr bǎi/liǎng bǎi	**ahr** by
500	wǔ bǎi	woo by
1,000	(yī) qiān	(ee) chee-en
first/second/ third . . .	dì yī/dì èr/ dì sān . . .	dee **ee**/dee **ahr**/dee **sahn**

USEFUL PHRASES

Hello/How are you	nǐ hǎo/nǐ hǎo ma?	**nee** how/ nee how mah?
Do you speak . . . . . . English?	nǐhuì shuō . . . . . . yīng wén ma	nee **hway** shwo **yeeng** wen mah?
I don't understand.	wǒ bù dōng	woh **boo** dohng
I don't know.	wǒ bù zhī dào	woh **boo** jer dow
I am lost.	wǒ mílù le	woh mee loo luh
What is this?	zhè shì shén me	juh shur **shun**-muh
Where is . . .	. . . zài nǎr?	. . . **dzy** nahr?
the train station?	huǒ chē zhàn (zài nǎr?) . . .	who-**oh** chuh jahn
the subway station	dì tiě zhàn . . .	dee tee-**ay** jahn . . .
the post office	yóu jù . . .	yoh jew . . .
the bank	yíng háng . . .	**yeeng** hahng . . .
the hospital	yī yuàn . . .	yee yoo-**en**
my hotel	wǒ de bīn guǎn . . .	woh duh **been** gwahn . . .
I am American	wǒ shì měi guó rén	wo **shur** may gworen
British	yīng guó rén	**yeeng** gwo ren
Australian	ào dà lì yà rén	ow dah lee yah ren
Canadian	jiā ná dà rén	jee-**ah** nah **dah** ren

Where are the . . . rest rooms?	cè suǒ zài nǎr?	**tsuh** swoh zy nahr?
Left (side)	zuǒ (biān)	zwoh (bee-**en**)
Right (side)	yòu (biān)	yoh (bee-**en**)
In the middle	zài zhōng jiān	zy johng jee-**en**
I'd like a room	wǒ xiǎng yaò yī ge fáng jiān	woh shee-ahng yow ee guh **fong** jee-**en**
I'd like to buy . . .	wǒ xiǎng mǎi . . .	woh shee-angh my
How much is that?	ná duō shaǒ qián?	nah **dwoh** shao chee-**en**?
A little	yī diǎn	ee dee-**en**
A lot	hèn duō	hun **dwoh**
More	duō	**dwoh**
Less	shǎo	shao
I feel ill	wǒ bù shū fu	woh boo **shoo** foo
I have a problem	wǒ yǒu yī ge wéntì	woh yoh ee guh **wen** tee

AT THE RESTAURANT

Where can we find a good restaurant?	Zài nǎr kěyǐ zhǎodào yìjiā hǎo cānguǎn?	**dzy** nahr kuh yee jow dow **yee** jee-ah how tsahn gwahn?
We'd like a(n) . . .	Wǒmen xiǎng qù yì	woh mun shee-**ahng**
restaurant.	gè . . . cānguǎn.	chew yee guh . . . tsahn gwan.
elegant	gāo jí	gow jee
fast-food	kuàicān	**kwy** tsan
inexpensive	piányì de	pee-**en** yee duh
seafood	hǎixiān	hy shee-**en**
vegetarian	sùshí	soo shee
Café	Kāfēi diàn	kah fay dee-**en**
A table for two	Liǎng wèi	lee-**ahng** way

index

FODOR'S POCKET SHANGHAI

EDITORS: Carissa Bluestone, Amy Karafin

Editorial Contributors: Laurel Back, Paul Davidson

Editorial Production: Kristin Milavec

Maps: David Lindroth, *cartographer*; Bob Blake and Rebecca Baer, *map editors*

Design: Fabrizio La Rocca, *creative director*; Tigist Getachew, *art director*; Melanie Marin, *photo editor*

Production/Manufacturing: Yexenia (Jessie) Markland

Cover Photograph: Bill Bachmann/Network Aspen

COPYRIGHT

Copyright © 2002 by Fodors LLC

Fodor's is a registered trademark of Random House, Inc.

All rights reserved under International and Pan-American Copyright Conventions. Published in the United States by Fodor's Travel Publications, a unit of Fodors LLC, a subsidiary of Random House, Inc., and simultaneously in Canada by Random House of Canada, Limited, Toronto. Distributed by Random House, Inc., New York.

No maps, illustrations, or other portions of this book may be reproduced in any form without written permission from the publisher.

Second Edition

ISBN 0–676–90128–X

ISSN 1520–4952

IMPORTANT TIP

Although all prices, opening times, and other details in this book are based on information supplied to us at press time, changes occur all the time in the travel world, and Fodor's cannot accept responsibility for facts that become outdated or for inadvertent errors or omissions. So always confirm information when it matters, especially if you're making a detour to visit a specific place.

SPECIAL SALES

Fodor's Travel Publications are available at special discounts for bulk purchases for sales promotions or premiums. Special editions, including personalized covers, excerpts of existing guides, and corporate imprints, can be created in large quantities for special needs. For more information, contact your local bookseller or write to Special Markets, Fodor's Travel Publications, 280 Park Avenue, New York, NY 10017. Inquiries from Canada should be directed to your local Canadian bookseller or sent to Random House of Canada, Ltd., Marketing Department, 2775 Matheson Boulevard East, Mississauga, Ontario L4W 4P7. Inquiries from the United Kingdom should be sent to Fodor's Travel Publications, 20 Vauxhall Bridge Road, London SW1V 2SA, England.

PRINTED IN THE UNITED STATES OF AMERICA

10 9 8 7 6 5 4 3 2 1